This is an excellent [illegible] ed-
ibility, sensitivity an [illegible] ith
in Jesus Christ. She [illegible] and
her wide experience [illegible] other people's lives with deep and profound biblical teachings. I highly recommend this book to everyone, especially the singles and those who minister to them. I believe you will find this book helpful and enlightening.

Datin Julia Yong
Wife of Bishop Yong Ping Chung
2nd Archbishop of the Province of Southeast Asia

Four reasons why I wholeheartedly endorse and commend this labour of love: its biblically sound perspectives; Mary's humour and wit (I love the coping strategies she proposes); the spectrum of true stories of singles from which to draw inspiration or warning; and the gentleness with which such sensitive matters are handled.

Rev. Joshua Sudharman
Pastor, St. John's-St. Margaret's Church
Singapore

The Single's Connection is a must read for women, parents, husbands, pastors and anyone involved in singles ministry. Packed with strong biblical teachings and gems from experience, Mary Tay succinctly deepens our knowledge and helps us to better understand the single women in our family and church today.

Rev. Lewis Lew
Youth Pastor, St. John's-St. Margaret's Church
Singapore

Mary Tay's personal experience enables her to address the issues of being single with much depth, candour, empathy and humour. In this frenzied world of quick fixes and self-help prescriptions, what the single woman needs is a book that will keep her steadfast to her purpose, on her journey to become the woman that God intended her to be. I believe that this book will be a valuable resource for that journey.

Sarah Yong
30++ , Junior Church Counsellor

Mary Tay draws on timeless biblical wisdom and sensitively applies it in an Asian context. This wisdom is equally applicable in the West. The outworking may be different but the principles remain. Here is someone who has learnt the way to contentment, walking hand in hand with God.

Auriel Schluter
Counsellor and Pastoral Worker

A timely blessing and an Asian treasure! Written by someone who has journeyed with God, *The Single's Connection* discusses many issues that single women face in today's world. The book draws readers to God, the Perfect Lover, reminds singles of their identity in Christ, and brings hope to broken relationships.

Florence Lang
Single, 20+

I agree wholeheartedly with Mary that male pastors "who are married but not very much in touch with their own feelings or those of their wives" really do need to read this book! In addition to providing readers with a fresh and insightful Asian perspective on the subject of woman singleness (for which I believe many married men are largely quite clueless about, me included!), this helpful book handles the issue in a way which distinctly reflects Mary's trademark style — biblically centred and deeply personal — thus making it a most informative and enjoyable read. This book is highly recommended!

Stanley Tay
Family Life Ministry Pastor, St. John's-St. Margaret's Church
Married with two teenage daughters

What sets this book apart is its wider Asian perspective. Single women from any Asian background will identify with it and find it useful. Easy to read, insightful, candid, and biblically sound, this book deals with real and current issues of singleness sensitively. It also speaks to the heart.

Angie Tan
Single, 40+, Working in a cross-cultural situation

The Single's Connection adopts a holistic, Bible-based approach to singleness in which the author passionately engages her readers with well-authenticated real-life stories of women from different backgrounds and experiences.

Ling Kay Bin
Single, 60+, Retired School Teacher

THE SINGLE's CONNECTION

Transforming Relationships for Single Women

Dear Ruth,

"Made in the image of God"
and "Accepted in the Beloved"
- may these axioms be with you
always!

Mary W J Tay

Mary
14 May 2010

GENESIS

Genesis Books
An imprint of ARMOUR Publishing Pte Ltd
Kent Ridge Post Office
P. O. Box 1193, Singapore 911107
Email: mail@armourpublishing.com
Website: www.armourpublishing.com

14 13 12 11 10
5 4 3 2 1

Printed in Singapore

ISBN 13 : 978-981-4270-97-7
ISBN 10 : 981-4270-97-0

Dedicated to my dear niece
Faith Tay Say Luan,
A young widow

May God's love embrace you
May His strength sustain you
May the Power of the Resurrection
Make all things new for you

Contents

Foreword

I was in my twenties, still single and suffering a broken tooth. My mother's colleague kindly arranged a dental appointment for me. On my return from the dental clinic, my mother was questioning me more about the dentist than the dental treatment itself. Then it dawned on me that the whole episode was a clandestine matchmaking operation. Here I was opening my mouth to someone who was eyeing me with more than professional interest! Fortunately for me, that was my mother's first and final attempt at arranging a blind date.

Many years have since passed. But this incident flashed in my mind when Mary approached me to write a foreword. I count it a privilege to be entrusted by my sister-in-law to write this foreword. For her, what qualifies me for this task is that I have spent more than the first half of my life as a single before I married her brother, Moses.

As a committed Christian, I believe that Paul's injunctions in 1 Corinthians 7 are abiding principles to navigate life's journey. How do I dream dreams, yet pursue God's destiny for me and live a life devoted to pleasing God? In your hands, you are handling a book that will help you to do so. True to her academic background, Mary has presented us with a clear and comprehensive treatise carefully and cogently written. From her lifelong experience of being a friend and counsellor who lends a sympathetic ear to many, she has distilled precious insights into this simple but sincere soul-searching guidebook, full of deep spiritual nuggets and significant practical applications. More than this, she has shared candidly her own personal journey in the obedience of faith.

Read on and explore the dream to live as a significant single. Reflect and experience breakthroughs in your life situations. Be renewed and revived as you enter into the heart of the Heavenly Father, and His plan and purpose for you.

My prayer for you is that as you engage with this book, you will receive the truth that sets you free from the baggage of past hurts and the bondage of lies. May you also receive the grace that imparts healing and wholeness, the grace that enables you to live the abundant life as a beloved child of God.

Mrs Cynthia Tay
Wife of Bishop Moses Tay
1st Archbishop of the Province of Southeast Asia

ACKNOWLEDGEMENTS

This book could not have been written without much help. First, I want to thank my God for seeing me through many years of singleness. Some of these have been very difficult; others have been filled with joy. He is the one who gently pried open my heart and filled it with His love so that I can 'speak the truth in love' to others on the very sensitive topic of singleness. I realize that I am not a finished product, by any means. So if there are any remaining rough edges, just hang a sign "Work in Progress" over them.

It would be impossible to remember and give the names of every single woman who has shared her story with me over the years. The most significant of these have been featured in the case studies cited in this book but many others have undoubtedly affected my thinking about singleness.

I am deeply grateful to my sister-in-law, Cynthia Tay, for encouraging me to write this book and for writing the Foreword. I also thank her for the tagline to the title of the book.

Julia Yong, wife of Retired Archbishop Yong Ping Chung, gave so generously of her time in reading through the outlines, the entire manuscript, and even made long-distance calls to give me her comments. I am deeply indebted to her for all these and also for her commendation.

Sarah Yong, my tenant, graciously lived with the birth pangs of this book. I thank her not only for her flexibility in creating space for me to work on my book but also for loaning me many books on singleness, for her comments on both the outline and the final draft, and for her commendation.

I thank Joseph John for helpful discussions on singleness from a man's point of view and for loaning me his Powerpoint slides, books and papers on singleness.

I am grateful to the following who read the outlines to my book and gave me helpful comments: Amy Lau, Lewis Lew, Sita Shanmugam, Mogan Mannar, Rachel Lee, my nephew David, and my brother John.

A special word of thanks is due to those who undertook the mammoth task of ploughing through the unshortened draft and gave me helpful comments. They are: Joshua Sudharman, Lewis Lew, Angie Tan, Clare Cox, Michael Tan, my brother John, my sister Elizabeth, and Auriel Schluter.

My heartfelt thanks go to those who wrote commendations for the book: Julia Yong, Sarah Yong, Joshua Sudharman, Lewis Lew, Stanley Tay, Ling Kay Bin, Angie Tan, Florence Lang, and Auriel Schluter.

Finally, I thank Christina Lim for the loan of many good books on singleness and the staff of Armour Publishing for their helpful editing and for printing the book in good time. Any omissions or errors are, of course, my own responsibility.

Mary W J Tay

Introduction

There is no shortage of books written in English about single women. Websites abound to help them find husbands.[1] So why write yet another book on this subject?

PURPOSE

The purpose of this book is to help the single woman live life to the full. Whether young or old, never married, divorced or widowed, she can discover the 'joy of living' that God has intended for her. Marriage may come her way and she should be completely open to this possibility. However, singleness is not a consolation prize, a second best or a reject shop. Contrary to popular opinion, she is not incomplete unless she has a life partner. Her completeness does not depend on her marital status, but on her connectedness first with God and then with the people in her network of connections.

SCOPE

The focal point of this book is relationships. It covers a fairly wide range of issues that single women have to face in living out these relationships.

Focus on Women

Although some of these issues may also be relevant to single men, I have chosen to focus on single women for two main reasons.

First, I am a woman and have been single for a long time. I can make some claims about having an 'insider's view' of what it is like to be a single woman. However, I do not have the same depth of insight into single men.

Second, in many parts of Asia today, most people still hold double standards – one for men and another for women – when it comes to singleness and family life. For example, it is commonly thought that a man is still marriageable even in his forties, but the same is not true of women. The reason for this is because women who are past their child-bearing age (conservatively fixed at forty) are generally considered not marriageable any more but men can father a child even when they are in their seventies!

Asians also generally accept the fact that a man may re-marry when his wife dies or leaves him, but it is much more difficult for a woman to re-marry soon after the death of her husband or after divorce. She is somehow expected to be strong and raise her children without the support of a husband whereas husbands are not expected to know how to care for young children except with the help of a wife!

Focus on the Biblical Perspective

This book advocates family values from the biblical perspective that I have embraced all my life and has enabled me to experience forgiveness, peace, joy and love as a single woman living in Asia. As a result of adopting this particular perspective and because of constraints of space, nothing will be said about single women who are lesbians. This is a significant omission but I have made the choice to be silent on this topic as it is fraught with controversy in the world today, even more so in Asia, and an informed discussion of this topic would require much more space than is available in this book.

Focus on Relationships

It is my firm conviction that the main key to living a happy life is not money, marriage nor even meaningful pursuits. The main key is relationships. Men and women were created for a relationship of love, first with God, the Creator, and then with other men and women. When such relationships are broken, happiness cannot be found. Many of the beliefs expressed in books and blogs about being single fail to acknowledge this as the key to happiness, both for the married and the single woman. The title of the book, *The Single's Connection*, was thus chosen to highlight the central focus of the book – that the single woman needs to be connected in a healthy way to God, and the people she lives and works with.

Essential Keys to Healthy Relationships

The word 'relationship' has come to acquire a wide range of meanings in the world today. This book defines it from the biblical perspective. It spells out what God, the most important player in life, has to say about relationships. In my personal reading, reflections and responses to my own singleness, I have discovered some very important keys that God has given single women for living life to the full. Many of these keys have not even been mentioned in the literature on singleness. Others have only been discussed superficially.

The key for each chapter directs the development of the chapter. It also helps to clarify the meaning of some commonly misunderstood concepts, such as intimacy and where to find it, the distinction between loneliness and solitude or aloneness, and so forth. These are the keys to each chapter:

1. Identity: Who am I?
2. Identity: What am I looking for?
3. Beauty in widowhood
4. Beauty in divorce
5. Beauty in the 'never married' state
6. Surrender
7. Boundaries
8. Channel
9. Giving
10. Wholeheartedness
11. Power
12. Godliness
13. Contentment
14. Delight

Focus on Asian Perspectives

Here is a further distinctive of this book. Most of the published views about singleness have been expressed by women from the West, or by Asian women with a Western education and perspective. Many family traditions and expectations arise from fairly conservative Asian viewpoints even in the more Westernised nations in Asia. An understanding of these traditions and expectations should help single women cope better with the pressure to get married. For example, many marriages in Asia are still the result of efforts to match single women with prospective life partners.

Focus on Case Studies

The final distinctive in this book lies in the many case studies of both happy and unhappy single women in Asia. In the course of my travels throughout Asia, and in my role as teacher and confidante to many younger single women, I have noted their thoughts, emotions and reactions as they journey through singleness. Each story in this book is a true story that serves to illustrate the point being made. However, in order to protect the identity of the one whose story is being told, and because the story can only be told in part, the names given are not the real names of the women.

Who Should Read This Book?

Single women should read the book. Single men might find it helpful.

Married people might wish to read this book to get a better understanding of what single women experience in their journey through singleness. Some married people, especially those who married young and are happily married, are often quite unaware of the struggles that single women go through. They sometimes make seemingly innocent and complimentary remarks like, "What's such an attractive woman like you doing still single?" or "How come you are not yet married?" The implications behind these comments are very hurtful because the first implies that attractive women get married and unattractive ones do not, and the second that it is only a matter of time before a woman gets married. Such unhelpful comments continue to circulate in Asian communities today, despite the fact that the number of single women in Asia today is rising.

Parents who are anxious about their daughters being unmarried, divorced, or widowed would also benefit from reading this book. By putting pressure on their daughters to get married, at whatever cost, parents sometimes drive their daughters to marriages that end in divorce. It is hoped that anxious parents may learn something about how to help their unmarried daughters in their singleness.

But perhaps the ones who most need to read this book are male pastors and counsellors who are married but not very much in touch with their own feelings or those of their wives. By focusing their ministry on families and ignoring the needs of many singles in their churches, many have continued to contribute, unintentionally, to the 'woundedness' experienced by single women. My hope is, therefore, that pastors will also read this book and begin to think creatively and constructively, if they have not yet done so, about how to develop a community of love and intimacy for Christian single women in their churches. As for counsellors and mentors of single women, I hope that after reading this book, they will gain some fresh insights about how to journey with their counselees in a more Christ-like way.

1

ISSUES OF IDENTITY

In some countries in Asia, we have to carry identity cards to show who we are. These cards identify us according to certain criteria which are considered important in the country that issues it. For example, the identity card for Singapore citizens has the following information on it: an identity card number, name, race, date of birth, sex, residential address, and even blood group! Whether it is to open a bank account, to process a housing loan or simply to get a discount off a bill, such cards are indispensable as a means of identification.

A single woman's identity is the master key that unlocks fullness of life for her. What are the most important issues of identity for her?

WHO AM I?

Perhaps the most important marker of an Asian woman's identity is whether she is married or single. Among the singles, further distinctions need to be made between those who are widowed, divorced or never married as the issues of identity that they face are different. Despite the large numbers of single men and women living in the cities of Asia, and the high rates of divorce, most Asians (for that matter, most people) still tend to assume that everyone should be married by a certain age.

How do single women respond to this assumption? Two case studies serve to underline different responses. First, there is the story of Rosemary, a single woman in her late fifties. She gets really irritated when someone addresses her as Mrs without first verifying if she is married. Her usual sharp response is, "I am Miss, not Mrs. Must everyone be Mrs?" This only invites even more caustic replies like, "Yes, you should be Mrs by now because of your age!" Rosemary finds that neither singleness nor age appears to be on her side.

The other case study is that of my own response. When I was in my early forties, I took a year's sabbatical leave overseas. One of my colleagues from Singapore expressed shock, surprise and disbelief when she found out that I was not married. She thought I was joking and insisted that she had read about me in the local papers – that I was married to a brilliant brain surgeon and had two equally brilliant children. I thanked her for her good wishes but assured her that the brain surgeon existed only in her brain and not in my life. She had made the wrong assumption that I was married because of my age and even read someone else's story into my life.

We cannot change other people's expectations of us but the key to our own happiness lies in our response to these expectations. If we live to meet only other people's expectations, we set ourselves up for a life of failure, misery and lack of fulfilment. If we live for ourselves alone, we become selfish, bitter and lonely. The key to happiness lies in knowing who we really are.

In Asian Society

In traditional Asian society, women were trained, from a very young age, by their own mothers to become good wives and mothers. The seriousness and thoroughness of such training is based on the premise that a woman's whole purpose of existence is to serve her husband and children. For many centuries, this was simply accepted and never questioned.

Today, however, many Asian women, married or single, would not subject themselves to such 'domestic' training so readily. Instead, they rebel against the idea that their identity comes from being a good wife and mother. Others have developed a new understanding of motherhood and partnership in which domestic skills are perceived as less important.

In Asia today, many women resist being identified purely by their marital status. Instead, they seek their own identity by making outstanding contributions at work, in society and even in church. They seek to become 'somebody' rather than just 'so-and-so's wife'.

In Asian society, whether its traditional values have been eroded by global influences or by time itself, a single woman, like any other human being, works out her identity through the complex network of relationships that she is part of. Although she herself may be Western-educated, those in the society in which she lives may not be. Misunderstandings and unhappiness often arise as a result of the 'conflict of values' between East and West. The issue is not whether Asian or Western values are superior. The issue is how to build good relationships in a cross-cultural, inter-generational and even multi-religious household.

In Asian Families

For the single woman living in an Asian family, there is a whole network of relationships with her family of origin that may seem to remain constant throughout her life. However, the shape of these relationships inevitably changes with the seasons of life as parents get older and die, siblings get married, nieces and nephews are born, grow up and get married, and the next generation of grandnieces and grandnephews is born.

The single woman needs to consider how best to relate to her family of origin for these family relationships are inescapable markers of our identity.

Daughter to Parents

In Asia, it is quite common for unmarried daughters to live with their parents. In such cases, it is important for them to develop their own identity apart from their parents.

However, a family nucleus with both parents living happily with their unmarried daughters(s) is becoming rarer even in Asia, as the number of unwed mothers and divorces increases. Increasingly, among those who are now in their early teens, many will grow up to be daughters of single parents. These will certainly perceive their identity as 'daughter to parents' in different light.

Sister to Siblings

Unless we are an only child, we would probably have at least one or more siblings. Depending on whether one or both parents remarried after being divorced, widowed, or whether they had other children outside marriage, we will need to learn to relate to all these siblings, regardless of whether we share the same parents or not.

One dimension that makes the relationships with siblings a challenge is when a sibling gets married. Continuing good relationships with them and their spouses presents new challenges and calls for greater understanding than before.

Aunt to Nieces and Nephews

In Asia, many unmarried aunts may have the opportunity to develop good relationships with their nieces and nephews. Much depends on the relationship between the aunt and her married siblings. When these are strong, healthy and supportive, it seems natural, in Asia, for a married sibling to ask his or her unmarried sister to play a major part in the life of her nieces and nephews. This may involve anything from providing transport for tuition classes to cooking their dinner when the maid is off, to checking on their school work, and even letting them spend their holidays with the unmarried aunt so that the parents can take a break.

Unmarried aunts who relate well to their nieces and nephews may be identified as 'so-and-so's aunt,' an extension of their identity in the family which they may welcome.

Grandaunt to Grandnieces and Grandnephews

Unmarried aunts who have established good relationships with their married nieces and nephews will find themselves invited to participate in the lives of their children. By the time grandnieces and grandnephews come along, the chances are that the grandaunt will be nearing retirement, if she has not already retired. Many single women dread retirement if they have not developed hobbies during their working life or if they have not established good relationships outside their immediate workplace. For those who have taken the time and trouble to nurture their family relationships, their identity is further enhanced when they come to be known as 'so-and-so's grandaunt.'

In Christ

Your identity as a member of your family of origin may be a happy or unhappy one. If you have grown up in a broken family, you may not want to bother with family relationships. If you have been sexually abused by your father or older brothers, you might find it more peaceful and less hurtful to keep to yourself, your own friends and your own life. You might prefer to just forget totally about family relationships. Below are two case studies of single women who grew up in dysfunctional families. Read them and judge for yourself what made the difference in their lives.

Roberta grew up in a home where her father constantly abused her. Every time she failed an examination, she would be caned until her flesh ripped apart. It was not because she did not work hard enough. She did but school work was just too challenging for her. She vowed to leave home as soon as she could and get married to the first man who was interested in her. She did so but within six months, the marriage fell apart. Today, Roberta is a broken woman, embittered by both her family of origin as well as a failed marriage. A Christian friend has repeatedly tried to share God's love with her. But Roberta has not yet opened her heart to anyone, not even to Jesus who has promised amazing grace and unending love to all who would follow Him.

Here is the second case study. Gladys also grew up in a dysfunctional home. She never really knew a father's love. Her parents had divorced just before she was born and her biological father never bothered to try to meet her, even after she had grown up. She knew what it was to be unloved but one Christmas, someone brought her to a church service and there she heard that Jesus could be everything that her family was not. She opened her heart to Jesus and life has never been the same again.

If you are in any way like Roberta or Gladys, even in the midst of your tears, anguish and despair, just know that a loving God has come in the person of Jesus Christ. Our earthly relatives may have disappointed, betrayed or failed us in many ways, but Christ has come to make us "a new creation" (2 Corinthians 5:17). He came so that we may "have life and have it to the full" (John 10:10).

The word 'Christian' as it is used in this book is defined not as a set of purely intellectual doctrines, or even a particular lifestyle, but as a person who has an ongoing, living, personal relationship with Christ. What makes this relationship so crucial to all our relationships is that Christ, the perfect lover, never fails us. No matter how many times we fail him, He never gives up on us. His beloved disciple, John, put it this way, "There is no fear in love. But perfect love drives out fear" (1 John 4:18).

The true identity of the single woman, like that of the married woman, is found in Christ. The two most significant markers of our identity in Christ are: who we are in Christ and whether we have received God's love.

Who We are in Christ

Best-selling author Neil Anderson, whose book *Victory over the Darkness* has helped many people step out of spiritual darkness into the light of God's amazing love, highlights who we are in Christ.[1]

I Am Accepted

John 1:12	I am God's child.
John 15:15	I am Christ's friend.
Romans 5:1	I have been justified.

1 Corinthians 6:17	I am united with the Lord, and I am one spirit with Him.
1 Corinthians 6:20	I have been bought with a price. I belong to God.
1 Corinthians 12:27	I am a member of Christ's Body.
Ephesians 1:1	I am a saint.
Ephesians 1:5	I have been adopted as God's child.
Ephesians 2:18	I have direct access to God through the Holy Spirit.
Colossians 1:14	I have been redeemed and forgiven of all my sins.
Colossians 2:10	I am complete in Christ.

I Am Secure

Romans 8:1, 2	I am free from condemnation.
Romans 8:28	I am assured that all things work together for good.
Romans 8:31-34	I am free from any condemning charges against me.
Romans 8:35-39	I cannot be separated from the love of God.
2 Corinthians 1:21, 22	I have been established, anointed and sealed by God.
Philippians 1:6	I am confident that the good work God has begun in me will be perfected.
Philippians 3:20	I am a citizen of heaven.
Colossians 3:3	I am hidden with Christ in God.
2 Timothy 1:7	I have not been given a spirit of fear, but of power, love and a sound mind.
Hebrews 4:16	I can find grace and mercy in time of need.
1 John 5:18	I am born of God and the evil one cannot touch me.

I Am Significant

Matthew 5:13, 14	I am the salt and light of the earth.
John 15:1, 5	I am a branch of the true vine, a channel of His life.
John 15:16	I have been chosen and appointed to bear fruit.
Acts 1:8	I am a personal witness of Christ.
1 Corinthians 3:16	I am God's temple.
2 Corinthians 5:17-21	I am a minister of reconciliation for God.
2 Corinthians 6:1	I am God's co-worker (see 1 Corinthians 6:9).
Ephesians 2:6	I am seated with Christ in the heavenly realm.
Ephesians 2:10	I am God's workmanship.
Ephesians 3:12	I may approach God with freedom and confidence.
Philippians 4:13	I can do all things through Christ who strengthens me.

Who we are in Christ does not depend on our marital status. We can do nothing to earn our identity in Christ. Neither can anything we do negate our position in Him, the position which He has secured for us through the death of Jesus on the Cross. However, in order to experience our true identity in Christ on a daily basis, we do need to 'receive' Jesus into our lives the way we would receive an honoured guest into our homes, with one notable exception. He is in fact our Creator and Owner and the more we release control of our lives to Him, the more wonderful life will be.

Have We Received God's Love?

Our identity in Christ is further strengthened when we receive God's love into our lives as the best form of love that we can ever experience. This applies not only to single women, whether they have never been married, are widowed, separated or divorced. It also applies to everyone. If we listen to the media, or read the best-sellers, we can easily be led to believe that the love between a man and a woman is the best form of love that anyone can ever have. But if we read the Bible, we will see beyond a shadow of doubt that God's love far surpasses that love.

There are at least two ways in which God's love surpasses marital love. First, it is everlasting. Marriages may be made in heaven but they end on earth. In a good marriage, there is much love but the marriage vows last only till death separates husband and wife. If a married woman has not learnt to lean on God's love, she can be in for a rude shock when her husband dies.

The second way in which God's love is even better than married love is that it is unfailing. Some of my married friends tell me about the promises that their husbands make but never keep. How it hurts when someone you love breaks a promise! In contrast, Psalm 6:4 says: "Turn, O Lord, and deliver me; save me because of your unfailing love." If we can rest on the assurance that God's love for us is both everlasting and unfailing, we have found our true identity in Christ and also our true love, whether we are married or single.

Deuteronomy 7:9 gives us another promise: "Know therefore that the Lord your God is God, He is the faithful God, keeping His covenant of love to a thousand generations of those who love Him and keep His commands." God's unfailing love is not conditional upon whether we are married or single. The only condition is that we should love Him and keep His commandments. Whether we are married or single, God has a plan for our lives. If we learn to love Him and keep His commandments, the promise of everlasting and unfailing love is ours to enjoy forever.

It would be good to evaluate where you are with the list above. Do you believe in the list at all? Do you truly believe it with all your heart? Or is it merely head knowledge? Your honest response to this list may well reveal any problems you may have with your identity. Do you have issues of security, significance and acceptance? Reflect on this and see if there is something you can do to settle these issues once and for all.

CONCLUSION

Our true identity comes not from WHO we are but WHOSE we are. The single woman who has found her identity in Christ is indeed a happy woman. Her position in Christ should give her the confidence that she has a place in her extended family and her community.

2

THE SEARCH FOR IDENTITY

Once a woman has found her true identity in Christ and resolutely refuses to conform to worldly models, half her battle has already been won. The other half of her battle with singleness has to do with her 'image'. A single woman needs to know how to handle the image that others have of her and her singleness, which may be flattering or faulty. But it is through the lens of her self-image and her true image in Christ that she can see herself as she truly is.

IMAGES OF THE SINGLE WOMAN

Flattering Images

Some people, especially those who feel trapped in a difficult marriage, envy the single woman. They have a flattering image of singleness. They think of singleness as 'pure bliss', a state almost like paradise where you can be totally carefree. They think that single women have all the time in the world and have more money. This image of singleness is too flattering. Any single woman can easily verify that singleness per se is neither perfect nor even much fun on some days.

These same people also tend to think that the single women have remained single by choice and offer superficial reasons for this state of singleness. They see young single women as being very fashionable, as belonging to the 'swinging' set who can party till all hours of the night, being very smart (too smart to get hitched), being independent and strong, and just 'living it up' every day. Ask any single woman and she can tell you that life is not uniformly wonderful just because she is single. Even living the high life can become tiring and may only awaken her inner desire to get married and to have someone cry with her in her frustrations and laugh with her in her joys.

Faulty Images

Other people, especially those who are happily married, cannot see singleness as being good for anybody. They tend to have a faulty image of singleness and single women. They think of singleness as a besieged city and the singles inside as desperate to get out. As the case studies in this book reveal, there definitely are singles who are desperate to get married but for as many 'desperate to get married' singles, there are probably as many 'contented' singles.

Another faulty image is that most 'normal' women get married and only in exceptional circumstances should they stay single. This image is faulty because the assumption behind it is that there is something not quite 'normal' and hence something 'wrong' with being single. There may indeed have been hidden fears, bad experiences and other reasons which were indeed 'wrong' and had these been resolved, they might have got married. But that is a separate issue.

This question "Is there something wrong with me?" is among the five most common questions that single women ask God and struggle with in different ways through the different seasons of their singleness.[1]

A faulty image of singleness, one held especially by single women themselves, is that a woman is not 'complete', that there is something missing in her personhood, as well as in her life, until she gets married. Many Asian communities do not consider people as adults unless they get married. Imagine how difficult it is for a 60-year-old to be treated as still a child or a minor just because she is not married! The Bible teaches that we are 'complete in Christ Jesus'. We do not become complete through marriage. We are already complete in Him.

Self Image – Is There Anything Wrong with Me?

In an article in *Christianity Today* that discusses the toughest questions singles ask, the second question deals with haunting, sometimes unanswerable, questions such as "Is there something wrong with me?" or "Am I not married because of past mistakes?"

The article in *Christianity Today* gives a good answer to this question. "As for the question about there being something wrong with you – well, ultimately the answer to that question doesn't matter. There's something wrong with everyone, married or single. 'For all have sinned…' (Romans 3:23). If there is something about you that's a hindrance to marriage, God can take care of it, no matter what it is. Ask Him to address any issue that may be standing in the way. Then yield to Him when He does. True peace and contentment come when we focus our attention on God's ability to resolve problems more than on our tough questions."[2]

As singles, we can choose to do nothing about our low self-image by continuing to believe that there is something wrong with us just because we are not married. Or we can open our hearts to what the Bible teaches us about our true image in Christ, regardless of whether we are single or married.

True Image

Our true image about our identity in Christ has already been mentioned in Chapter 1. The question is, how do we choose to see ourselves each day when the desire to get married lingers lovingly in our hearts, but the biological clock is ticking away and time is not on our side?

What mirror do we use to see ourselves? We can choose to see ourselves through the mirrors that others have of us. The result of this choice would be disappointment and low self esteem. But we can also choose to see ourselves through God's mirror for us which is clear, sharp and unchanging.

In a very insightful drama, entitled 'Mirrors,' Bob Snook demonstrates how seeing our true image in God not only rids us of our poor self-image but also all the other distorted images, whether they be flattering or faulty ones.

Then I began reading my Bible and there was a new image. The image is not distorted or dark like the other mirrors. It's clear and sharp and unchanging. It doesn't rely on the opinions of others. It doesn't depend on what I've done or what I've left undone. It's my image as God sees me. If I trust Jesus for my future, I'll be able to see things the way they really are. No expectations, no disappointments, no deficiencies. How can that be?! What makes me look so good here, when I was so distorted before?

Now it's clear. Yes. It's clear. I was made in the image of God himself, with no distortion at all.

I guess that's why I finally stopped worrying about all those other images and started concentrating on God's image of me. [3]

THE SEARCH FOR IDENTITY

Beauty

Single women today are prepared to invest a lot of money and time to look good. Not only does looking good give women confidence, some even feel that our identity is somehow bound up with our looks. Some claim that we feel better if we look good. Certainly the media sends out the message that good-looking women are the ones who attract men, land that highly sought-after job, model success, drive flashy cars and live in luxurious condominiums. However, whether such attraction culminates in a happy marriage, and whether fast cars and high profile living brings happiness is quite another story.

It is so easy for women to get caught up in the pursuit of worldly beauty. Franklin puts it so well. "Women strive to shape their lives after that which popular culture tells them is beautiful, and Christian women are no exception. When we are preoccupied with physical attractiveness, we assert that the world's standards of beauty matter more than God's, and we begin to reflect the values of a world that Jesus said we are not a part of even though we remain in it."[4]

The single Christian woman living in Asia today needs to answer this question for herself, "Is there anything wrong with the pursuit of worldly beauty?"

In keeping with the biblical perspective adopted in this book, we shall look for our answer from the Word of God itself and not from beauticians and the wisdom of the world.

In his high-priestly prayer in John 17, Jesus prayed, "I do not pray that you should take them out of the world, but that you should keep them from the evil one. They are not of the world, just as I am not of the world" (John 17:15, 16) (NKJV).

What is the world that we are not to be part of? Scripture gives the answer. "For all that is in the world – the lust of the flesh, the lust of the eyes, and the pride of life – is not of the Father but is of the world" (1 John 2:16) (NKJV).

John defines 'worldliness' in terms of the deadly trio – 'the lust of the flesh, the lust of the eyes, and the pride of life'. This trio characterises a life lived according to the expectations of the world, not a life lived according to the Father's wishes. Not only does this lethal trio draw us away from God, they also attract lustful looks from men which may lead to lustful words and actions.

Some single women may be a bit naïve but the vast majority subtly invite men to lust after them by the way they dress. Except for Muslim women who cover themselves from head to toe, most 'modern' women dress to expose a lot of flesh and to accentuate a 'sexy' figure. If a single woman succumbs to 'the lust of the flesh' by the way she dresses, can she blame men for roving eyes and roving hands?

Then there is 'the lust of the eyes'. Men are sexually tempted and led astray by what they see. King David's adultery with Bathsheba started when he saw her bathing and he noted that she was beautiful. If a woman exposes those parts of her body which should be reserved only for her husband's eyes, she is seeking to bring glory to herself and her own good looks. At the same time, she is inviting the kind of attention from men which can progress from a glance to a lingering look, to a burning desire which is restless until he has her completely to himself, and this may happen outside marriage.

What about 'the pride of life?' The Bible shows us how we are to use our bodies as the temple of the Holy Spirit. What is required of temples is cleanliness and holiness, not dazzling beauty. Modesty in clothing is the responsibility of every Christian woman. Some women dress to attract men, who in turn are drawn not to love them but to lust after them. Let each single woman search her own heart and try to answer the following question, "Does the way I dress lead a man to draw closer to God because of the godliness he sees in His temple (my body), or does it tempt him to want to see more of my 'flesh'?"

Indeed, the single Christian woman who has found her true identity in Christ needs to shut off the voices of society and her own voice which persistently invite her to pursue the path of worldly beauty. Again, Franklin puts it so well.

> "The Christian woman hears the voices of society and the voices within her own heart and mind. She knows that true meaning comes from someone outside of this world. She knows that true life is found in Christ. Often, however, she compartmentalizes her life. She can accept Christ as her righteousness in regard to her sin, but she has difficulty conceptualizing Christ as her beauty."[5]

Fame

Some single women know that they will never find their identity through their physical beauty. So they try to find it through fame. They seek to excel, to make a name for themselves in something – whether it is in cooking or flower arrangement or in their studies or sports. When they become well-known in some area, they feel that they have found their identity as they are now known as 'somebody' and not just 'anybody' or 'nobody'.

Fortune

Yet other single women know that they are neither beautiful nor able to make a mark in any area of their lives. But they are good at making money. So they focus their energies and time on amassing wealth. They become 'rich' and 'famous' because of their wealth. But the path of 'fortune' is a slippery one. We have seen all too clearly how those who have depended on their 'fortunes' to give them their identity in life have faded into oblivion almost overnight in an economic meltdown.

Marriage

Less educated single women may be less independent. Rather than seek their own identity, they seek it through marriage. They cannot wait to be known as 'Mrs So-and-So', especially if that 'So-and-So' is also good-looking, rich and famous! This search for one's true identity through marriage is not a good reason to get married. The many and varied emotional needs of a woman cannot be completely fulfilled in just one man, although in a good marriage, many women have found what they were looking for. Marriage, like singleness, is a precious gift from our Creator who can 'craft' our marriage or our singleness to something that is 'just right' for us.

Love

The human heart longs for love in a way that must have been implanted in our lives by God Himself who is Perfect Love and the Perfect Lover. St. Augustine, one of the early church fathers, looked for love in all the wrong places for many years by following his heart's desires. He pursued the love of women and even had an illegitimate son. It was only when he turned his back on his immoral life and turned to God that he realised who the real 'love of his life' was. In a prayer which has now become well-known throughout the Christian world, Augustine said, "You made us for yourself, O Lord, and our hearts are restless until they have found their rest in you." King Solomon also pursued the love of women – he had 700 wives and 300 concubines but despite this, he found life 'meaningless' when life is lived without God.

Some single women, hoping to find their true identity through being loved, have become disillusioned when that love is not strong or permanent enough for a commitment in marriage. Although some single women may proudly boast that "it is better to have loved and lost than not to have loved at all," they may never have recovered from the sense of loss. They are unable to live life to the full as the shadow of regret seems to hover over everything they do. Single women who have never dated or lost a boyfriend may feel deprived in their weak moments. But if they have guarded their own hearts and willingly kept their emotional space only for their God, they do not need to live in regret.

ACCEPTING OUR TRUE IDENTITY

As a Woman

"What is the true identity of a woman, compared to the identity of a man?"

Let us find some answers to this question from the Bible itself. Genesis, the first book of the Bible, explains how God created the heavens and the earth, the animals, and finally men and women. A key verse that sums up God's creation of men and women is Genesis 1:27 (NKJV):

> "So God created man in His own image,
> in the image of God He created him,
> male and female He created them."

What does this verse teach about the identity of men and women?

First, both men and women were made in the image of God. It is this common 'designer-made' characteristic of both men and women that sets us apart from the animals. We are made in the image of God. We have built-in capacities for love and intimacy. We have built-in capacities to worship God in a way that the animals do not have.

Unfortunately, this image of God in women has been badly tarnished over the centuries by men oppressing women, seeing them only as sex objects and keeping them in a position subordinate to men. Even today, many young girls, and even little children, are sold as sex slaves throughout Asia.

The image of God in men has also been badly tarnished especially by women who, in their enthusiasm to 'right the wrongs' of the past, have forgotten that men, like them, were made in God's own image as well. Their feminist militancy has not only robbed men of their confidence but has even instilled in some men the 'fear of women' instead of the 'fear of God'.

Restoration to the true image of God is possible and has been offered to us as a free gift through Jesus Christ. But it can only be restored His way, by repentance, both by men and women coming to the Cross. It is only when we are ransomed, healed, restored, and forgiven by surrendering our fractured lives to the Saviour who died in our place that we find our true identity as women. Crucifying men for their sins only leads to more hurts.

The second important principle that emerges from Genesis 1:27 is that God made men to be men and women to be women. God created two distinct sexual orientations: male and female. Any other orientation is nothing short of a total disorientation that robs us of our true sexuality.

The third principle that needs to be highlighted is that men and women were created to come alongside each other, to complement each other and not to compete against each other. Eve, representing all women, was 'designer made' because God realised that it was not good for Adam to be alone and because he could not find 'a helper suitable for him' among the animals (Genesis 2:18-20).

It is significant how God created women and where they came from. Eve was made, not from Adam's head so that she might fight with him over who the head was. Neither was she made from his feet so that he could trample her underfoot. Instead, God in His sovereign wisdom, made Eve from Adam's rib, at his side. She did not come from a subordinate position and should not fight her way to the top. In Christ, men and women are heirs together of the grace of God, joint-heirs with Jesus Himself.

Debates about the equality of men and women seem to miss a very important point. The issue is not equality but complementarity. If men and women devoted their energies to complement each other in the best way, whether in the context of marriage or in team work in the marketplace, more men would fulfil their God-given destiny as men and more women would fulfil their equally God-given destiny as women.

As a Single Woman

Here are some reasons why many single women feel unloved and unaccepted in 'a couple's world':

1. Well-meaning friends and relatives sometimes say to singles, "How come such a nice girl like you is not married?" The implication is, of course, that nice girls get married and those who are not nice (in one way or another) do not manage to get married.
2. The single woman may have had one or more broken relationships. She may have been jilted by her boyfriends time and again. The breakups may not be entirely her fault but it is easy to conclude that there must be something wrong with her for so many men in her life to have abandoned her.
3. She may not have had any dates at all. Unless she is very confident and secure in her own worth and has a healthy self-esteem, it is natural to conclude that no man has ever been attracted to her because there is something wrong with her.
4. The voices of those nearest and dearest to her – her own family members – may have been mainly, if not entirely, negative. "You are so hot-tempered! Which man wants to marry you?" or "Try to make yourself look more presentable or no one will ever ask you for a date!"

5. Voices within persistently try to breathe lies to us. They tell us negative things about God – that God has forgotten about us, that He does not hear our prayer for a husband, that He does not really care how we hurt when we see others happily married, and so on and so forth. They distort our true image, the biblical image that we have been made in the image of God, whether we are married or not.

God is the only one who can see from the beginning to the end. Even when we have developed a close walk with God, we can only see darkly, as through a glass. All will be revealed on the final day when we meet Him face to face. It is so important to silence the destructive voices within us. Let me quote Franklin on this. "We have listened to these messages and obeyed them for so long that they have taken root in our hearts and become the words by which we live – words of inadequacy, failure, ugliness. They are the lies that we know better than truth."[6]

LIVING WITH THE PRESSURE TO GET MARRIED

Although every Christian woman knows in her mind that God loves her and has plans to prosper her, to give her a future and a hope, her heart does not always so readily accept that it is better to remain single than to marry the wrong man. There are several reasons why this is so.

First, there is internal pressure. Every woman has probably dreamt of her Prince Charming in his shining armour coming to claim her for his own. For some, this may only have been a childhood dream. But many women continue to feed these dreams by watching romantic movies or reading love stories, and so they keep alive the desire to get married, the desire, so they think, to finally find fulfilment in life.

Second, there is the continuous pressure from parents and family members. Most of the time, the pressure is born out of concern for the unmarried daughter or sister. It is difficult for any parent to see his or her unmarried daughter getting older each year and not interested in getting married. Even Singapore's highly revered Minister Mentor Lee Kuan Yew has admitted publicly his concerns for his unmarried daughter, Lee Wei Ling.[7]

Third, there is pressure from society. The world has changed quite a bit in its views towards singleness. When I was a young adult, it was just assumed that everyone would get married, notwithstanding the shortage of Christian men who were available for Christian girls to marry. The pressure to get married was intense. Today, the pressure from society has eased quite a bit but is still present in parts of Asia.

Fourth, there is even pressure from governments. For example, the Singapore government has repeatedly sounded alarms about what society would become if more and more people refuse to marry or have children. It was a great relief to most single women in Singapore when Lee Wei Ling, the daughter of MM Lee, wrote frankly about the reasons why she is single and happy to be single. [8]

Finally, dating agencies and the 'matchmaking' arm of some churches put a certain kind of pressure on those who use their services. Dating agencies are under pressure to produce results, usually measured by the number of marriages they manage to arrange. The single woman who desires to get married should use dating agencies with caution. She may well find her future husband through them but it would be sad if she gets married just because she cannot take the pressure any more.

The pressure to get married will always exist in Asian societies. It is how we handle these pressures that will make or break us. Below are two case studies, one of a woman who could not take the pressure of her mother's constant nagging to get married, and the other of one who resisted the pressure to get married and remained single.

Anna was a very attractive young lady who had a brilliant academic record. She fell in love with a fellow undergraduate but he was not ready for marriage and showed no interest in her. In the meantime, her mother kept putting pressure on her to get married as she was not getting any younger. Along came an older man with all the spiritual qualities that she was looking for, and he swept her off her feet. They were married after only a short acquaintance. They brought into their marriage unresolved hurts and finally divorced after many long years of bitterness.

Julia was an equally brilliant student but without Anna's good looks. Like Anna, her mother also put a lot of pressure on her year after year to get married. When she went overseas to do postgraduate work, she fell in love. It was a cross-cultural relationship but that was not the problem. However, as they got deeper into the relationship and considered marriage, Julia became very concerned that she would be disobeying God if she married him as he did not have a personal relationship with God even though he went to church. Regretfully, they realised that they did not have enough in common to build a strong marriage. So they broke off the relationship. It was a mutual decision but not without its hurts. It was years before he finally got married. She has remained single and has come to accept her singleness as God's gift to her.

LIVING IN THE LIGHT OF ETERNITY

Some of us reading this book may never become brides. We may become bridesmaids many times over but not brides. However, for those of us who have entrusted our lives with Jesus, there is one wedding that we can look forward to. It is THE wedding of all time! He is coming back on the final day to meet us just as a bridegroom meets his beloved bride at a wedding.

How do we prepare ourselves for that ultimate wedding feast? In processing the desire to get married, let us not miss the ultimate purpose of why we are here – that we might be invited to the marriage supper of the Lamb of God.

Living in the light of eternity is not just a pious platitude. It is a reality that can be a daily experience for every single Christian woman who truly loves her Lord. In the words of Kane,

> "To be filled with faith in God, have the hope of an eternal perspective, and be filled with His love to share freely with others can then defeat our fears of failure, rejection, abandonment, and death."[9]

Let God and the eternal perspective rule our lives and we will experience unending joy. But let fears rule our lives and we will be crippled for life. The choice is ours to make.

CONCLUSION

A single woman may never become another man's 'special woman' in the context of marriage. But we can certainly become God's 'special woman', 'one after His own heart', and the bride of the Lamb of God.

The most important characteristic of our identity is who we are in Christ. No matter how society or others view singleness, security comes from being ransomed, healed, restored, and forgiven by Christ and from being in Christ.

You are unique. When God made you, He did not clone you, or mass-produce several like you. Before you were born, the Lord thought of you, loved you and created you in your mother's womb, just so that you could be you. Far too many women drive themselves to become like several of their role models all lumped into one body. To have such 'noble' ambitions is actually to court disaster.

A well-meaning friend once sent me this message as a New Year greeting. "In the New Year, may you seek the patience of Noah, the faith of Abraham, the submission of Isaac, the perseverance of Jacob, the forgiveness of Joseph, the meekness of Moses, and the courage of Joshua. May you run the heavenly race with Jehovah as your shepherd." I said 'Amen' to the last statement about running the race with God as my shepherd, but I certainly did not think that the Good Shepherd would expect me to live out the lives of seven men! Rather, in seeking to become God's woman, my greatest need is to sit quietly, without fretting and without restlessness, at His feet and listening to His words.

3

Seasons of Singleness: Widowhood

Apart from identity, another important key that unlocks fullness of life for the single woman is the key called Seasons. The Bible teaches us clearly that there are times and seasons for everything. Understanding that seasons may not last forever helps us to go through the season we are in, especially if it is a difficult one. As Solomon, one of the wisest men who ever lived, put it so eloquently:

> There is a time for everything,
> and a season for every activity under heaven:
> a time to be born and a time to die…
> a time to weep and a time to laugh,
> a time to mourn and a time to dance…
>
> a time to embrace and a time to refrain,
> a time to search and a time to give up…
>
> **(Ecclesiastes 3:1, 2, 4, 5, 6)**

We were all born single and when we die, we have to make the journey on our own, whether we are married or single. In that sense, singleness is a season of life for everyone. For some, singleness may be a short season because they get married young and stay married a long time. Or it may be a short season in old age when they outlive their spouse. For others, it may seem like a long winter especially if they never recover from widowhood, divorce or a broken engagement. For those who are enjoying their singleness, the season may seem like eternal spring. But for those whose desire to get married does not diminish over the years, the season may seem long and filled with anxiety. It is like waiting at a departure lounge for a flight to take off. All we hear are repeated announcements of further delays until the flight is finally cancelled.

As a season of life, singleness may mean different things to different women. But the woman who has found her true identity in Christ knows in her heart that it is God who makes 'all things' beautiful in HIS time.

WIDOWHOOD

Some women are single because of the death of their husbands. This kind of singleness, or widowhood, is the kind that is most easily understood and accepted by other people. It is understood because it fits in well with societal expectations that marriage is the norm and that change in marital status caused by death is no one's fault unless, of course, murder or suicide is suspected. The divorcee who loses her husband through divorce may be plagued with questions, spoken or otherwise, like "Whose fault was it?" and "Why did it have to happen?" But the widow often receives concern and sympathy.

GOD CARES FOR WIDOWS

In the Old Testament, God is portrayed as one who "defends the cause of the fatherless and the widow, and loves the alien, giving them food and clothing" (Deuteronomy 10:18). The psalmist praises God for "The Lord watches over the alien and sustains the fatherless and the widow" (Psalm 146:9). The major prophets – Isaiah, Jeremiah and Ezekiel – in pronouncing the sins of the people single out their failure to "bring justice to the fatherless, and plead the widow's cause" (Isaiah 1:17, 23; Jeremiah 7:6; 22:3, Ezekiel 22:7).

God's provision for the widow is seen in the detailed instructions that He gave to the people of Israel about how to protect and care for them.

1. If her husband dies without leaving her children, the husband's brother should marry her and produce offspring for his brother. In this way, not only will his brother have offspring, but the widow herself will not be left defenceless, with no husband and no children to protect her.
2. In giving the laws about social justice to the people of Israel, God warned them not to mistreat widows or orphans (Exodus 22:22), otherwise their wives would become widows and their children fatherless (Exodus 22:24b).
3. Any vow or obligation taken by a widow or a divorced woman would be binding on her (Numbers 30:9). In other words, she is to be treated as seriously as if she were married, with a husband to speak on her behalf.
4. The provision that God made for widows was not made out of pity. He reserved the best for them. For example, they were entitled to the same food as the Levites – God's special chosen race of priests (Deuteronomy 14:28, 29; Deuteronomy 26:12, 13).
5. The widows, fatherless and aliens were included in the many feasts and celebrations when food was abundant, for example, at the Feast of Weeks (Deuteronomy 16:11) and the Feast of Tabernacles (Deuteronomy 16:14).
6. In the instructions for harvesting, specific provision was made for leaving something for the aliens, the fatherless, and the widow so that "the Lord your God may bless you in all the work of your hands" (Deuteronomy 24:19).
7. The one who withholds justice from the alien, the fatherless or the widow is actually cursed in Deuteronomy 27:19, along with other curses in the list of curses and blessings.

THE ROLE OF THE CHURCH IN CARING FOR WIDOWS

The care of widows had always been a priority among God's people (see Exodus 22:22; Psalm 68:5; Isaiah 1:17; Acts 6:1-6; 9:36-41; James 1:27).

The proper and equitable care of widows caused the first major disagreement in the Jerusalem church (Acts 6:1). Guidelines were needed for the Ephesian church. Paul wanted to deal with the younger widows, who might have been among those drawn away by the false teachers (2 Timothy 3:6). He contrasted them with other – usually older – widows, whom he classified as 'really widows' (1 Timothy 5:3, NKJV).

In 1 Timothy 5:3-16, Paul gives the following advice about how the church should recognise the needs of widows, the criteria to use in determining which widows to help and why, and also the behaviour expected of widows who are Christians.

Those who qualified for assistance from the church were:
widows genuinely in need (5:3, 5, 16);
without family and friends to care for them (v. 4, 5, 8, 16);
godly, praying widows (v. 5, 9, 10);
old enough to make remarriage unlikely – over 60 years (v. 9).
Paul advised the "younger widows" to remarry and
to become godly wives and mothers (v. 11-15).

LESSONS FROM WIDOWS IN THE BIBLE

The Widow of Zarephath (1 Kings 17)

The unnamed widow in this story illustrates the sad plight of many widows. She had no one to care for her and she had to provide for a young son. When the prophet Elijah came to her, she was facing one of two terrible prospects. Either she would have to watch her child die of starvation before her eyes or if she died first, her son would be left without love and care. She was a Phoenician and had no claim upon Israel's God. When speaking to Elijah, she referred to God as "the Lord your God" (1 Kings 17:12).

Elijah's request that she make him a small cake before she prepared food for her son and herself must have seemed utterly outrageous to her. She had barely enough for herself and her son to have their last meal and yet he asked to be fed first! Despite her abject poverty, she did as she was told. She put the needs of the man of God before her personal needs. We cannot be sure what motivated her to obey Elijah. But whatever it might have been, the Bible makes one thing absolutely clear. This simple act of faith on the part of the widow opened the floodgates of heaven. From then on, the flour and oil never ran dry – a sign that the Lord provided for her needs, just as Elijah had promised.

This widow learned to trust God during those days. The days of trusting God for daily provision surely must have made it a bit easier for her to follow the prophet's instructions. Her joy at seeing her son restored to life was crowned by a deeper degree of faith in Israel's God, the Provider for all who trust Him (see Luke 4:25, 26).[1]

There are many useful lessons for widows in this story.

1. God provides for the basic physical needs of widows, whether or not they know God personally. He sent one of His chosen prophets to her, even though she did not know God and even though she had nothing to offer.
2. God also provides for the emotional needs of the widow. When her son died, He used Elijah to raise him back to life and to bring him back to her. He was all she had. He would be her sole breadwinner when he grew up.
3. Learning to trust God in hopeless situations strengthens our faith.
4. God uses widows to accomplish His higher purposes. God had earlier used ravens to feed Elijah but when the brook dried up, He commanded the widow to feed him. What a privilege to serve a man of God in this simple way!
5. If we give to God all that we have and obey Him before meeting our own needs, He will multiply our limited supply of resources.

6. Anger that is released to God opens channels for God's mercy to flow through. The widow's deep sense of loss at the death of her son triggered anger and she blamed Elijah for the death. But God did not punish her for this because in her anger, she turned to God's servant for help.

Ruth, a Young Widow (Ruth 1-4)

One of the most well-known and well-loved stories about widows found in the Bible is the story of Ruth, the great grandmother of King David and an ancestor of Jesus Christ, mentioned by name in His genealogy (Matthew 1:5).

Ruth was a young widow from Moab. Out of sheer love for her widowed Israelite mother-in-law, Naomi, she abandoned her own culture and followed Naomi back to the land of Israel after her own husband died, leaving her without any children. She said to Naomi, "Your people will be my people and your God my God" (Ruth 1:16). By so doing, she was actually cutting off her chances of remarrying an eligible young man from her own community.

Once she was back in Bethlehem (which means 'the house of bread'), she worked hard to provide for her own physical needs and that of her mother-in-law. She went out and worked as one of the labourers reaping the harvest. It was back breaking, the weather was hot and as, a young woman, she faced some risks as the men could have taken advantage of her (Ruth 2:9). She did not take things for granted. She did not expect things to just drop from heaven without hard work. It was as she was working hard in the fields day after day that Boaz, a distant relative, noticed her. He was attracted to her by her loyalty to her mother-in-law, her disposition and character. Nothing is said about her physical beauty. The story concludes with Boaz taking Ruth as his wife and they became King David's great grandparents.

The story of Ruth is a model for young widows in the following ways.

1. She 'clung' to her mother-in-law as she identified totally with her. This loyalty to the only living relative of the 'family' she married into is outstanding and praised by all in the story. Ruth's story is also a story of a good cross-cultural marriage.
2. She did not seek remarriage as her first priority or a right, even though Naomi and everyone else expected her to remarry one of her own people back home. She was certainly still young enough for that to happen. That was probably the reason why her sister-in-law, also a young widow, left Naomi and we never hear of her again.
3. Ruth's loyalty to her mother-in-law arose out of her loyalty to God. "Your people will be my people and your God my God" (Ruth 1:16).
4. She followed God's plans for her to marry a kinsman-redeemer[2] even though Boaz was probably old enough to be her father! She did not go after young men, whether poor or rich, but waited patiently for God to bring His chosen life partner into her life. It was through this older man that she became an ancestor of Jesus.
5. God can be trusted to provide another life partner for a young widow, if that is His plan for her.
6. What drew Boaz's attention to Ruth was not her beauty but her godly character and her dedication to her mother-in-law. If she had spent all her time beautifying herself in trying to attract the attention of men, she would have attracted the 'wrong' men, and missed out on God's will for her to become an ancestor of Jesus Christ through her marriage to Boaz.

Anna, an Old Widow (Luke 2:36-38)

Anna, a prophetess, was married only for seven years and she was a widow until she was eighty-four. She never left the temple but worshipped night and day, fasting and praying. She came up to Mary and Joseph just as they were presenting the eight-day-old Jesus for circumcision and prophesied about the child to all who were looking forward to the redemption of Israel.

In these three short verses, we catch a glimpse of what Anna's widowhood was like. It was a life lived not in 'solitary confinement' in the temple, but in 'solitary refinement'[3] as God prepared her to release the word of prophecy at the right place and the right time.

There are three lessons that widows can learn from Anna:

1. A life of solitude need not be a life of loneliness. Anna was alone but not lonely. She established deep intimacy with God.
2. Her life was a life dedicated to God (v. 37). She never left the temple; she worshipped day and night; she fasted; she prayed.
3. Her life was one in which God's gifts could grow. At the age of 84, she was still exercising her gift of prophecy. She spoke about the child Jesus and what He would mean to "all who were looking forward to the redemption of Israel."

ACCEPTING YOUR SITUATION AS A WIDOW

Below are three case studies of women who have not merely accepted their lot in life as widows but are radiant examples of how God works all things together for the good of those who truly love him.

A Story of Grief Re-made into Joy

Eunice lost her husband in the first year of their marriage. He was taken seriously ill on their honeymoon itself. For the next few months, she looked after him tirelessly. They fervently prayed for a miracle but he died. She went through the various stages of shock, denial, loss, grief, guilt and even shame for a few years but today, although she has not remarried, she is at peace as a widow. While she is open to remarriage, she considers as her first priority being a 'bride of Christ'. She was only a young Christian at the time of her husband's death, but the amazing grace of God and the love of her church family saw her through the 'fiery furnace' when her faith was sorely tested. Today, she radiates with joy because "joy is sorrow inside out, grief remade again."[4]

A Story of Loss Re-made into Care and Counsel

Charis became a young widow, with two young children of pre-school age, when her husband died. Like any other widow, she experienced grief and loneliness. But she devoted her energies to bringing up her children in the fear and love of God. By the grace of God, she succeeded. Today, both her children are married and have their own families, and she remains close to them.

Today, Charis is an intercessor and a counsellor. She is able to intercede effectively for people as she has learnt to discern the voice of the Good Shepherd through all her confusion, pain and suffering. She is able to counsel well as she is able to empathise with others.

A Story of Loneliness Re-made into Active Cross-cultural Work Overseas

Samantha was already in mid-life when she was widowed. She and her husband had been married for many years. They were childless and the death of her husband left an aching void in her heart and a loneliness that just would not go away. Years after he died, she was still wearing her wedding ring and she often talked about her husband as if he was still alive. She lived in the past and had the posture of a widow in mourning – both in the clothes she wore and in her general demeanour.

Her church family, knowing the shock and grief that she was still experiencing, never judged her. They did not ask her 'to snap out of it' in an insensitive way. They let her mourn her husband's loss for quite a few years. But they subtly began to provide opportunities for her to serve. Slowly but surely, she learned to let go of the past as she shifted her focus from herself to the needs of those she was serving.

As she found new meaning in life, she removed his photograph from their sitting room, and her wedding ring from her finger. She did not re-marry but the Lord called her to missions and she is now very active in cross-cultural work in East Asia. Having experienced deep pangs of loneliness, she is a welcome companion to those who are on their own, without family and close friends, in the mission field.

DEALING WITH TROUBLESOME EMOTIONS

A change in marital status, especially a sudden one, is never easy to accept. It is especially difficult in the following situations:

1) Prolonged Illness

After a woman's husband dies of illness, one question that can continue to haunt her is, "Did I do enough for him? Or was I too busy with my career, caring for my children and my elderly parents?"

2) Unexpected Death

When her husband dies suddenly, unexpectedly, when he is still in the prime of life or after a short illness, a woman finds herself suddenly alone and having to face a complexity of tasks and feelings never before experienced.

The emotions that accompany the loss of a spouse are: shock, grief, blame and forgiveness. It is only when she has dealt with these 'troublesome' emotions that resolution and the rebuilding of her life can begin. The journey to full recovery may be a long and painful one.

One of the most helpful books about the nature of grief is C.S. Lewis' *A Grief Observed*, which describes how he felt when his wife died. Reading it will help us see that it is normal and quite acceptable to God to feel the way we feel in grief. The Psalms, especially the lament psalms, also show us how to take our negative emotions to God, to talk to Him and even to yell at Him in anger.[5] Through such 'crying out loud' to God, we ultimately gain a fresh perspective of God. We may never have our 'WHY' questions answered but by talking to Him, we will discover a fresh perspective of WHO He is, and this perspective will give us the courage to get on with life.

H. Norman Wright, in *Let's Just Be Friends* talks about some necessary steps towards recovery – giving yourself time, cleaning up memory lane, letting go and grieving.[6]

According to Wright, there are six stages of grief:

- Stage 1: shock
- Stage 2: grief
- Stage 3: blame
- Stage 4: forgiveness
- Stages 5 and 6: resolution and rebuilding

These stages may not occur chronologically but in cycles. The widow must not be surprised to be visited by cycles of grief or unforgiveness before she finally recovers.

Stages 3 and 4 are particularly relevant in sudden death. It is quite common for a bereaved wife to blame the medical professionals, the medication, even herself and the caregivers for not being vigilant enough (although they probably could not have done anything about it). Where the widow finds herself blaming someone, including herself and even God, for the death of her husband, she needs to forgive them before she can rebuild her life again. Grief affects different people differently. Some, regardless of their spiritual maturity, may take much longer to recover from the grief. We must respect this and not try to 'fast-forward' the whole process of healing.

Further details of how to handle each of these stages are found in Wright's book.

The importance of handling these negative emotions well is underlined in the following quote:

> "Death has a way of changing our lives forever. Pretending things are the same would keep us stuck in our grief. Refusing to go on would mean our families lost not only one person, but lose us as well. Acceptance is necessary if we want to resume our lives."[7]

MAKING ALL THINGS BEAUTIFUL IN WIDOWHOOD

The three case studies of real, living Asian widows given above illustrate not only their acceptance of widowhood but also how they allowed God to make all things beautiful in their season of singleness.

The importance of family and the Christian community cannot be underestimated. They are often the ones that God uses to bring comfort to widows in their mourning, encouragement in their depression, faith to replace their fears and insecurities, and hope to build a future for themselves and their children.

But ultimately, while others can journey with us in our seasons of grief and pain, it is only when we talk to God, telling Him honestly how we feel, that we can begin to change our perspective from our pain to WHO God is and His infinite love for us. Below are two specific ways in which God makes all things beautiful in widowhood.

Filling Emptiness

The loss of a loved one brings with it feelings of emptiness. It is when the widow releases her anxieties to God through prayer, obeys God in whatever He requires of her, and offers Him her emptiness, that He can fill her to overflowing so that joy might return to her life.

> "During intense grief, widows need intimate times with family. In quietness and seclusion, anxious hearts express heartache, fears, loss, and pain (Philippians 4:6). Communication flows; prayer times increase; God's plans are seen more clearly as He is allowed to fill our emptiness with Himself (Ephesians 5:17, 18).
>
> Often without realizing it, an outpouring of God's grace comes through obedience (2 Kings 4:5). No one is exempt from its overflow. Family and friends are touched by its reality. And hope is received through faithfulness in doing God's implicit will (Jeremiah 29: 11-14).

Offering empty vessels to God involves hands, bodies, brains, emotions, thoughts, dreams (Romans 12:1, 2). It is giving Him all we are, have or hope to be. Behind shut doors, we can immerse ourselves through His presence (Psalm 139:23, 24).

God could go on filling cleansed, empty vessels, but He knows just how much is needed (Philippians 4:6, 19). His ending of the flow is as deliberate as the beginning. His oil will always be in sufficient supply (2 Kings 4:6).

God's intentions for women emerging from the life-changing experience of widowhood and child-rearing are unlimited. He has provided material needs (2 Kings 4:7). And He has sent His Son that we might have life and that we might have it more abundantly (John 10:10). With the presence of God's Spirit within, widows can find new relationships and responsibilities, which should be accepted by them with great joy, realizing that each is a gift from God's heart (Ephesians 3:16-21)."[8]

Rearing Children Alone

Apart from needing to fill her own emptiness, the widow is often left with children whom she must bring up and care for, often with insufficient financial resources. Children tend to mirror the behaviour of the widowed parent. Where children have previously seen a parent growing in the Lord and being attentive to His Word, there will be a closer bonding as the family faces new realities (1 Timothy 5:4).

Children mimic parents. If the widow is a woman of faith, she need not be worried about her own future and that of her children. The faith of the prophet's widow in 2 Kings 4 reflected a continuation of the way she had lived before death took her husband. Her children knew well her deep commitment to God. Without questioning, they hurriedly joined her in following God's new instructions. Refusing to allow human anxieties and concerns to overshadow the providence and faithfulness of God, this woman heard Elisha's instructions and immediately went into action (2 Kings 4:5).

Widows often become very prayerful. Notice in the 2 Kings 4 story, that in the midst of the crisis, the widow and her sons expected God to answer their prayers (v. 5, 6). Nothing else had such importance to them (Psalm 146:9). Beyond each desperate need was the promise that the Lord would surely hear their cry and He did (Exodus 22:22, 23).

Widowhood gives the opportunity to trust God wholly and completely at a time when all earthly props seem to have been taken away (see Joshua 1:5-7, 9).[9]

THE QUESTION OF REMARRIAGE FOR A WIDOW

Marriage vows last only as long as both husband and wife are alive. In traditional Asian communities, while widowers are expected to remarry, the same does not hold true for widows. The woman who remarries after her husband's death is often judged to be doing something quite unnecessary as she is expected to devote all her emotional energies to her children. If she marries soon after her husband's death (for example, within a year), she would even be criticised for marrying with 'indecent haste'.

The Bible does not prohibit remarriage for a widow. However, a widow will need to consider at least three basic questions before she plunges into a marriage just to fill her own emptiness.

First, she should ask herself if she has allowed herself adequate time to grieve properly the loss of her husband, whether the marriage was perceived as a good one or not. A 'failed' marriage, coupled with the complex feelings of grief, guilt, etc., does not lay a good foundation for a second marriage.

Second, the widow who has children should seriously consider if they can accept a stepfather. This is particularly important if the children are still young as their own views of marriage may be shaped by how the mother handles widowhood. If she is a good role model for them, the chances of her children having successful marriages will be strengthened. If not, their own marriages in the future may suffer as children typically reflect the values of their parents, especially in marriage.

Third, if the widow is a leader, she needs to consider if her remarriage would stumble the weaker ones in her community of faith. While she may have recovered from her own grief, especially if a man comes along and showers attention upon her, her relatives and friends who know her deceased husband may need a little longer to accept the changes because of their loyalty to her husband. While she does not need to seek approval or permission from them, she needs to prepare them for it.

CONCLUSION

As a season of singleness, widowhood may be experienced early or late in a marriage, when the woman is young or old, whether she has children, or not. In the case of sudden or unexpected death, she may feel overwhelmed by the emotions of grief, shock, blame and unforgiveness. But knowing how special a widow is in God's eyes, and how He will make all things beautiful in His time should give her the strength to accept this season of her life, and live life fully in peace and contentment.

4

Seasons of Singleness: Divorce

Age is no guarantee that a woman will be spared from divorce. There was a story told in the *Straits Times*, Singapore, of a 78-year-old woman who had been married for more than 40 years to the same man. Despite the long years of marriage, her husband wanted to divorce her. They had been separated for five years and he had since found a younger woman in her fifties to marry. Here is sad evidence of a marriage which had lasted for years but which may have gone sterile with unresolved marital conflicts over the years.

THE BIBLICAL PERSPECTIVE ON DIVORCE

The basic biblical teaching on divorce is found in Deuteronomy 24:1-4, Matthew 5 and Matthew 19. Below are some insightful interpretations of these passages.

Deuteronomy 24:1-4

This passage teaches about marriage and divorce. Although divorce, even at this time, was widespread (Leviticus 21:7, 14; 22:13; Numbers 30:9), it was never encouraged by God (Malachi 2:16). This case concerns remarriage after divorce. The 'uncleanness' referred to in the divorced woman cannot refer to adultery, for the penalty of adultery was death (Deuteronomy 22:22). It must refer to some indecent exposure or unwomanly conduct. The husband in such a case might choose to divorce his wife. Divorce was initiated by men, not women. If the woman was remarried and divorced again, her first husband could not remarry her because her remarriage after the first divorce would be considered adultery in the sense that she had lived with another man. This strictness on divorce would also stop wife-swapping and loaning for procreation or merely on a whim.[1]

Matthew 19

"In interpreting Moses' decree on divorce, Jesus did not go immediately to the contested text (Deuteronomy 24:1). Instead, He returned to the beginning of marriage (Matthew 19:4-6). Ultimately the answer to this problematic issue does not lie in legal codes, traditional practices or human solutions but in God's creative design (Genesis 2:24).

God never accommodates or compromises His principles, but He does redeem and restore all who seek His forgiveness.

Jesus' view of divorce can be understood only against the background of His view of permanent monogamy, one man and one woman together for a lifetime. The plan for permanence is clear in the 'one-flesh' metaphor used by the Lord. Moses allowed divorce as a human device to protect ill-treated Hebrew women from unscrupulous men who sought to manipulate the betrothal process. The Pharisees took the 'permission' of the Law and turned it into a 'command' that made human weakness an excuse for disobeying God's divine plan and purpose.

Jesus did not teach that the innocent party must divorce the unfaithful one. The purpose of the 'exception' clause in the Mosaic Law, which is repeated again in Jesus' explanation, is not to encourage divorce. The binding commitment of marriage does not depend upon human will or upon what any individual does or does not do but upon God's original design and purpose for marriage (Hosea 3:1-3).

God rejects divorce for these reasons:

1. Marriage is a divine institution the Lord used to teach His children about their relationship to Him (Genesis 1:27; Matthew 19:4).
2. Marriage is by express command of the Creator and carries His imprimatur (Matthew 19:4, 5).
3. Marriage brings two people together as one flesh, testifying to the permanence God planned for this most intimate union (Matthew 19:6).
4. Jesus points to the example of the first couple (Matthew 19:8).
5. Evil consequences are inevitable when separation comes (Matthew 19:9).

Divorce is never God's choice. Indeed, God hates divorce (Malachi 2:16). However, whenever divorce occurs, for whatever reason, God desires to work redemptively when the person who has experienced this tragedy is repentant and desires to be reconciled with God."[2]

Other biblical texts that are related to divorce are Exodus 21:7-11, Esther 1:10-22, Jeremiah 3:1, Malachi 2:14-16, Luke 16:18 and 1 Corinthians 7:10-17. Related topics are adultery (Hosea 3), commitment (Matthew 16), husbands (Job 31; 2 Corinthians 6), marriage (Genesis 2; 2 Samuel 6; Proverbs 5; Hosea 2; 2 Corinthians 13; Hebrews 12), remarriage (Matthew 5), vows (Numbers 30) and wives (Proverbs 31).

Increasingly, people end up being single because of divorce. This is nearly always accompanied by emotional turmoil and is difficult for all involved.

The two seasons of singleness discussed so far – widowhood and divorce – with their roots in loss, grief and suffering, can make the adjustment to singleness prolonged and painful.

ACCEPTING YOUR SITUATION AS A DIVORCEE

So, how does a woman accept her situation as a divorcee in the midst of her anguish? Below are the stories of two divorcees who have learnt to accept their situation in life.

A Journey from Denial to Acceptance

Beatrice could not believe her ears. Her husband just came home from work one day and announced that he wanted a divorce! She was a very easy-going woman who never demanded much from her husband. She never even questioned him about what he did and why he always worked overtime and was even away most weekends. They did not have any children of their own but her life revolved around the children in the orphanage she had started and she often neglected her husband.

Unknown to Beatrice, her husband was having an affair with a younger woman who was now expecting their first child. He wanted a divorce so that he could make a complete break with his wife and spend the rest of his life with his new-found love and the new family nucleus.

As a Bible-believing Christian, Beatrice felt that divorce was wrong and did not give in to her husband's repeated demands for a divorce. So the years passed. As she was getting near retirement, she suddenly realised that she had very little to live on. Her friends advised her that if the house was sold, she could at least have a lump sum and start life anew. After a prolonged time of praying and seeking the Lord, Beatrice finally and reluctantly agreed to the divorce. The sale of the property was settled amicably and she went overseas to start another orphanage.

Beatrice has since remarried. She has learnt many precious lessons from her first marriage. Things could have been different if she had spent more time with her husband. She also realised that spiritualising everything and just praying was not enough. Instead of denying that her first husband had really left her in every sense of the word, and denying that there was any problem with their marriage, she has learnt to accept her situation as a divorcee. She has forgiven her first husband, and her second marriage is working out much better as she has released her brokenness to the Lord and is learning to care for her second husband in a way that she never did with her first husband.

A Journey from Anger to Self-control

Deborah's marriage was a very stormy one from the very beginning. Both she and her husband had barely recovered from rejection when they got married. The man she had hoped to marry had disappointed her by being very indecisive and continuing to postpone their wedding date; the woman he was supposed to marry turned him down at the last minute because of parental objections. They were both fairly young and thought that there would be time to sort themselves out after they got married, since they both had experienced similar rejections. Their courtship was also a short one and they did not know each other well when they got married.

Soon after marriage, they had children. He did not take any interest in the children and it did not occur to Deborah to ask why until one day she suspected that her husband was having an affair with another woman. After a prolonged inquisition, he finally told her the truth – he had fallen in love with another woman. Shocked and angry, she started divorce proceedings against him and the divorce soon took place.

For many years, Deborah carried anger in her heart but she did not realise it. She was angry with God as they were both mature Christians when they got married and were so sure that they were meant for each other. Thus, when her marriage fell apart, she stopped going to church altogether. She rationalised that it was acceptable that she did not to go to church as she was too busy with her career and her children. She also cut herself off from her Christian friends as she felt that they judged her too severely and did not understand what she was going through. As expected, her spiritual health suffered.

However, God remained faithful to her. He brought new Christians into her life at her place of work and they lovingly nursed her back to faith. She learnt that she did not need to condemn herself as a bad Christian just because her marriage fell apart, that it was all right to release all her pent-up emotions to God, to have a good cry, and to release her brokenness to Him. She has not remarried, but her journey from anger to self-control has begun. She now lives with one of her married daughters who is so delighted to have her around. She is a very loving and patient grandmother to the grandchildren. She never scolds them the way she used to scold her husband and daughters. Instead, she exercises incredible patience and self-control in many situations.

DEALING WITH TROUBLESOME EMOTIONS

In addition to the emotions faced by widows, the divorcee may also need to deal with issues of unforgiveness, anger, bitterness and rejection.

Dealing with Unforgiveness

Unforgiveness is an emotion that confronts all seasons of singleness – whether a woman loses her husband through death or divorce, or when a never-married woman loses her fiancé or boyfriend through separation. However, as unforgiveness is perhaps the key emotion among divorced women, it will be discussed in this section.

First, there are a few myths about forgiveness that need to be debunked. Forgiveness is not saying a simple 'OK'. As we have seen from the preceding paragraphs, divorce is *not* 'OK' with God and with the divorced couple. Saying a simple 'OK' means "You didn't hurt me. You didn't do anything wrong. You didn't offend me."[3]

Forgiveness does *not* automatically restore a relationship. In the case of a divorce, restoration is seldom possible. Neither is forgiveness a complete forgetting. Where a divorced couple have been married for many years and have children, it is neither possible nor desirable to erase *all* memories of the past. As with all painful memories, we must seek God's cleansing power so that while the memories may remain, He will remove all the betrayal, pain, rejection, and hurts associated with the divorce. This may take time but it is God who makes ALL things beautiful in His time.

Second, forgiveness is impossible if we rely only on ourselves. There is much truth in the proverb "To err is human; to forgive divine." We all make mistakes without God's help but we cannot forgive without first receiving God's forgiveness and depending on Him for the power to forgive. Just as some Christians inscribe on their wedding cards, "We love because He first loved us," we need to inscribe in our hearts, "We forgive because He first forgave us."

The first step to forgiveness is to acknowledge that you have been hurt and that you need to forgive for the sake of your own physical, mental, emotional and spiritual health, not for the benefit of your ex-husband! As forgiveness is not a feeling but an act of the will, take some concrete steps to show God that you really want to forgive.

One possible course of action is that suggested by Wright.[4] He suggests that the person recovering from a broken relationship writes a letter to her ex, but not post it. In the first column, begin each sentence with "I forgive you for….", then go on to write down something that your ex did or did not do which still hurts and angers you. In the second column, write down the first thing that comes to mind. It may be an emotional rebuttal or protest that contradicts what you just wrote in column 1. For example, you might write in the first column, "I forgive you for not trying to make our relationship work." But you might write in the second column, "Why couldn't you have tried more? We might have made it!" These 'areas of forgiveness' may fill pages, but continue to do this prayerfully until your rebuttals in the second column change and finally disappear. That is when you realise you have really forgiven.

Another practical step is to erase the painful memories by getting rid of physical reminders of the memories. Except for the children of the divorced couple, almost everything else is disposable and the journey to total forgiveness is often made easier, for example, when the house is sold and the divorced wife moves to a different locality or to a different church (to avoid further gossip and prying eyes which inevitably slow down the recovery process) or even to a different country, as in the case of Beatrice discussed above.

Dealing with Anger

Anger, like many of the other emotions discussed in this section, is also an emotion that all singles have to face. In normal usage, the word 'anger' is used to represent many strong, negative feelings including extreme fatigue, extreme embarrassment, extreme frustration and rejection.[5] The divorced woman will probably experience all these feelings in the process of divorce. The root of her anger is being rejected by the man who once vowed to love her and only her till death separated them. Rejection will be discussed in subsequent paragraphs.

The Bible provides excellent instructions on the nature of anger and how to handle it.

Consider the following selection of verses and apply it to your own situation.

- "In your anger do not sin; when you are on your beds, search your hearts and be silent." (Psalm 4:4)
- "A fool gives full vent to his anger, but a wise man keeps himself under control." (Proverbs 29:11)
- "A man's wisdom gives him patience; it is to his glory to overlook an offense." (Proverbs 19:11)
- "'In your anger do not sin': Do not let the sun go down while you are still angry, and do not give the devil a foothold." (Ephesians 4:26-27)
- "But now you must rid yourselves of all such things as these: anger, rage, malice, slander, and filthy language from your lips.... put on the new self, which is being renewed in knowledge in the image of its Creator" (Colossians 3:8, 10).

The biblical perspective on anger is that it is sinful, foolish, and something to get rid of for our own good. The Bible does not recommend suppressing it or denying its existence as that is psychologically harmful, nor does it recommend its full release at specified targets indiscriminately. Instead, it teaches self-control and overlooking the offence. In other words, it is the way of the Cross as exemplified by Jesus Christ who cried out to God on the Cross, "My God, my God, why have you forsaken me?" (Mark

15:34) but bowed His head in submission to the Father as He willingly gave up His spirit in death that we might be saved from the punishment of our sins forever.

Here are some practical tips on how to release pent-up emotions of anger:[6]

1. Release your anger to God by talking to Him. Cry and scream if you want to, but take your anger to God and pray for His help in your situation. Some of the 'imprecatory' psalms, e.g. Psalm 13, may help you in this process.
2. Explain why you are so angry with your husband to a mature and understanding third party who will listen without condemning you and can advise you. A good person would be someone who has 'survived' divorce and come out of it without bitterness. The best would be someone who really exemplifies how God has made all things beautiful in her divorce.
3. Accept the fact that God has allowed the divorce to happen so that your character might be refined.
4. Acknowledge that you have imperfections which may have caused your husband to stray from you.
5. Realise that your husband's offence against you could not possibly equal your own guilt before a holy God. Yet He has forgiven you. Are we not obligated to extend the same mercy to others?

Dealing with Bitterness

One of the most comprehensive discussions on bitterness in single women is found in Clayton's excellent book, *Victory in Singleness.*[7] She gives a few key Bible verses about bitterness, real examples of women trapped in the bondage of bitterness, their struggle to break free from this trap, and practical steps to be taken, alongside Scriptural teaching, in the journey from bitterness to trust again.

Clayton's definition of bitterness is simple yet profound. "Bitterness is the baggage we carry when we can't get over something someone has done to us." It puts the onus on us rather than on the person or the circumstances that made us bitter. We are the ones who suffer because we cannot get over something and we are the ones carrying the baggage.

Clayton continues,

> "It bubbles up when we have been wronged or when life doesn't go our way. Bitterness is the intense feeling of resentment that arises out of an occurrence that is perceived to be an injustice. Not only is bitterness a feeling, but it is also a process. It is the gradual turning of our once warm hearts cold. The results of bitterness are seen in the withdrawing of love, the turning away from others, the protective walls we build around our hearts, and the unwillingness to trust."

Some of the symptoms of bitterness described by Clayton are:

- A tendency to be critical – we see what is wrong and we're quick to point it out.
- We talk about the faults of others – one of our favourite topics of conversation.
- We're overly sensitive and snippy.
- We second-guess people – we read into the actions of others and often misinterpret their motives.
- We have a hard time controlling our tone of voice when we communicate.

Bitterness is a disastrous situation to be in. We do well to heed biblical advice about bitterness. "See to it that no one misses the grace of God and that no bitter root grows up to cause trouble and defile many" (Hebrews 12:15). When bitterness takes root in our lives, it causes endless trouble – isolation, loss of identity and a lack of peace. It also defiles many as we can no longer trust nor receive love either from God or others.

How do we set ourselves free from bitterness? Clayton mentions three areas of trapped thinking that a bitter person must free herself from.

1. **I have a right to hold on to this grudge.** The divorced woman may feel that she has every right not to forgive her husband and 'the other woman'. She may be right. The question is: Does she want to remain in her prison of bitterness or walk out of it in freedom?
2. **God can't heal my broken heart.** The divorced woman may be trapped into thinking, "I trusted my husband completely but he betrayed me. How can I trust anyone again?" Yes, she can but she must allow God to heal her broken heart.
3. **God disapproves of me.** The divorced woman may convince herself that her husband left her because he disapproved of her in some way. And she may be right! But to conclude that God also disapproves of her is to make God like her husband. Instead, she must hold firmly to the belief that she is accepted by God even though He may not approve of the divorce.

Dealing with Rejection

Rejection is a difficult emotion for singles to deal with in all the seasons of singleness. I have actually heard grieving widows say such things as, "If my husband really loved me, he could have survived the cancer." and "How could he be so heartless as to leave me to raise two young children on my own?" Similarly, the wounds suffered by the never married whose boyfriend or fiancé left her are real and deep. However, the unkindest cut of all is probably the rejection suffered by a divorcee, especially after many years of marriage. So we shall deal with rejection in the season of singleness.

Derek Prince's highly readable book entitled *God's Remedy for Rejection* is perhaps the best book that I have read on the topic of rejection. In eight short chapters, he deals with the nature of rejection, the causes of rejection, betrayal and shame, the results of rejection, the ultimate rejection, how to apply the remedy, acceptance in God's family and the flow of divine love.

The divorced woman who is still suffering from the wounds of rejection by her husband will benefit from reading Prince's book. Our discussion on this topic will be limited to finding answers to three key questions:

1. What is the nature of rejection?
2. What are the results of rejection?
3. What practical steps do we take to be freed from rejection?

"Rejection can be defined as the sense of being unwanted. Closely related to rejection are the wounds of betrayal and shame."[8] The wounds inflicted by rejection are permanent. They are at the root of all personal problems. Prince asserts,

> "Sometimes rejection is so wounding and painful that the mind refuses to focus on it. Nevertheless, you know something is there – even though it is deeper than the mind, deeper than the reason, deeper than the memory. It is in your spirit."[9]

The fact that rejection must be understood in spiritual, rather than psychological, terms is well illustrated by the following verses from Proverbs:

> "A happy heart makes the face cheerful,
> but heartache crushes the spirit." (Proverbs 15:13)

> "A man's spirit sustains him in sickness,
> but a crushed spirit who can bear?" (Proverbs 18:14)

As for the results of rejection, Prince believes that "the primary result of rejection is the inability to receive or communicate love."[10] Besides an inability to show love, Prince discusses other secondary results as follows: "I would say that rejection produces three kinds of people: the person who gives in, the person who holds out, and the person who fights back."[11]

However, despite the disastrous results of rejection, Prince has good news for those who are suffering from the wounds of rejection. "God can heal you from the wounds that come from rejection, help you to accept yourself, and enable you to show His love to others."

Recovery from rejection involves taking two simple steps. First, recognising what Christ has done may bring release to some suffering from rejection. This recognition depends on facts and not feelings. The facts are that "Jesus provided healing for our wounded spirits through a series of exchanges on the cross. He was rejected by God and man in order that we might be accepted by God and God's family. He suffered shame so that we might share in His glory. He died our death in order that we might receive His life."[12]

Prince acknowledges that while recognising what Christ has done may bring release to some, others may need to take further steps:[13]

1. Letting the Holy Spirit help you identify how or where you have been wounded by rejection.
2. Forgiving the people who have harmed you (in this case, the husband and, if applicable, the other woman).
3. Laying down the destructive fruits of rejection such as resentment, bitterness, hatred and rebellion.
4. Accepting that God has accepted you in Christ.
5. Accepting yourself.

Question of Remarriage

Should a Christian divorcee remarry? This is a very difficult question to answer but some attempt will be made here to answer this question from a biblical perspective.

> "The Scripture lifts up permanent, monogamous union as the plan of the Creator (Matthew 19:4-6). To understand the strong language of Scripture concerning this matter, we need to look at the whole of Scripture to see how God regards marriage. The marriage bond between husband and wife is the same kinship bond that exists between parents and children, and between God and His creation (Genesis 2:24; Matthew 19:6)." It cannot be broken.

"Some argue that remarriage is never permissible (Mark 10:11,12). Others note that the teaching of Jesus on divorce includes an exception (Matthew 5:32; 19:9) and conclude that this implies permission to remarry. Still others suggest that the meaning of 'divorce' in ancient law included freedom to remarry, suggesting that remarriage is forbidden only after an invalid divorce.

Finally, there are those who deny that Jesus gives a justification for divorce in the modern sense, although they allow that remarriage is permissible if reconciliation with a divorced spouse is rendered impossible because of death or remarriage of the divorced spouse to another partner (1 Corinthians 7:10, 11) or if the divorced spouse is a non-believer opposed to reconciliation (1 Corinthians 7:15).

Despite these differences of biblical interpretation, some important conclusions can be drawn:

- Once remarriage follows divorce, there is no turning back (Deuteronomy 24:1-4). As the tearing apart of a marriage is painful, it leaves its scars on all who are affected by the tragedy.
- God sees the one-flesh relationship as permanent and binding because it is the picture He has chosen to portray His relationship to His children, and He guards the home with great zeal (Malachi 2:16).
- Jesus gives no divine directive nor even acceptable excuses for breaking this holy covenant but rather observes that the hardness of the human heart makes such tragedy a reality in this sinful world (Matthew 19:8).
- The role of the church and of believers must always be redemptive. With God, forgiveness is as if it never happened. No sin or tragedy is beyond God's forgiveness.

After seeking and receiving God's forgiveness, which all do repeatedly, a woman who remarries has a new understanding of God's incredible grace. She must then seek anew an understanding of God's plan for marriage (Genesis 2:24), commit herself wholeheartedly to pursuing His plan, and consider her vows of marriage binding before the Lord (Matthew 19:5, 6)."[14]

MAKING ALL THINGS BEAUTIFUL IN DIVORCE

Divorce leaves ugly scars which only God can remove. God makes all things beautiful, even through divorce. Some of the most beautiful women I know are divorcees who have every reason to remain miserable, and to continue to live with negative emotions such as bitterness and anger. But they have chosen, by an act of the will, to live in the present rather than in the past, to look to a future when they will be able to love and be loved again, to trust and be trusted. They know they cannot do this in their own strength. But faith in a good God and in the power of His Holy Spirit enables them to see their problems in perspective and to make a new start in life after divorce. In short, every spiritual blessing that God has promised to all His children is freely available to His divorced daughters as well. He grieves with them in their divorce but He does not love them less, nor will He punish them forever. He forgives divorcees who repent.

CONCLUSION

Divorce does not have to be a season of life. In dealing with divorce as a season of singleness, I am neither advocating divorce as a way out of a difficult marriage, nor am I distorting the biblical perspective of a 'one man – one woman marriage for life' by recounting stories of women who have allowed God to make all things beautiful in their divorce. If everyone believed that God's plans for a permanent, monogamous marriage are part of His creative design for men and women, and worked hard to make marriage succeed by practising forgiveness the way that Christ did, divorce would never take place.

However, as divorce is a painful reality of life and is now widespread even among Christians, I have chosen to deal with it, even though it is a thorny issue. I have made this choice in the hope that singles would not rush into marriage thoughtlessly, and those already married would do everything that is humanly possible to strengthen and heal marriages in trouble, by fervently asking God to do the naturally impossible.

5

Seasons of Singleness: The Never Married

When women today say that they are single, they generally mean that they are not currently in a sexual relationship. The current usage of the phrase 'never married' rarely means 'never had sex'. Some younger single women experiment with same sex relationships. Some try many and varied means of having a baby without a permanent, monogamous marriage to a man, claiming that they just want to experience motherhood which they consider desirable, regardless of whether they are married or not. Today we can no longer assume that a single woman who has never been married has no children.

What are we to make of such thinking and behaviour? Once again, I believe that the Bible provides much sane advice to a world that has gone 'sex-crazy' and satisfying answers to what the 'never married' woman is looking for.

THE BIBLICAL PERSPECTIVE ON THE UNMARRIED

Matthew 19:10-12

In Matthew 19:10-12, the disciples said to Jesus, "If this is the situation between a husband and wife, it is better not to marry." Jesus replied, "Not everyone can accept **this word**, but only those to whom it has been **given**. For some are eunuchs because they were born that way; others were made that way by men; and others have **renounced marriage because of the kingdom of heaven.** The one who can accept this should accept it."

There are two main points in Jesus' teaching on singleness here:

1. Singleness is a gift for some, just as marriage is a gift for others.
2. Celibacy may be a choice that is made for the sake of the kingdom of heaven.

1 Corinthians 7

This chapter gives Paul's personal views about marriage, divorce and unchangeable circumstances. The Corinthians are commanded to be faithful in their marriages, to avoid divorce and to be content in their calling – whether to marriage or singleness.

"I wish that all men were as I am. But each man has his own gift from God, one has this gift, and another has that. Now to the unmarried and the widows I say: It is good for them to stay unmarried, as I am. But if they cannot control themselves, they should marry, for it is better to marry than to burn with passion" (1 Corinthians 7:7-9).

Paul highlights the fact that both marriage and celibacy have their own benefits, and both should be considered gifts. He is happy that God has given him the gift of being content with remaining unmarried, since this permits single-minded devotion to the Lord's work (v. 32–33, 40). Remaining unmarried is a gift that many others do not have. See v. 28, 36; Matthew 19:12.

From the two passages cited above, we derive the most important perspective that the Bible offers to the 'never married': singleness is a gift and a calling from God.

While it is clear that the Bible teaches that singleness is both a gift and a calling from God for some, there are many unmarried women who see it as a gift that they would rather not have.

Some worry about remaining single when they don't have the gift. Such worry is often based on a wrong understanding of the character of God – that He would give us a gift that we cannot accept. Somewhere in our hearts and minds, we have stopped believing that God is good and that He loves us in our singleness.

We may also be deceiving ourselves in saying that we don't have the gift when in reality it is basically an unwillingness to accept the gift of singleness. We are unwilling to grow, to learn God's ways and to submit to His plans for our lives. Instead, we insist on pursuing our own plans, whatever it may cost us in the long run. We are wise in our own eyes.

Another reason why many unmarried women cannot see singleness as a gift is because they are not experiencing joy and victory in handling the challenges of being single. It is to these challenges that we now turn.

CHALLENGES FACED BY THE UNMARRIED

Sense of Belonging

One of the challenges faced by the never married is her sense of belonging. There is a very real sense in which a married woman feels that she belongs to her husband and her children. She has 'someone to come home to' every day at the end of a hard day's work in the marketplace, or someone to come home to her if she is a homemaker. For the never married, however, there can be no such sense of belonging.

Leigh McLeroy in her book entitled *Moments for Singles*,[1] speaks of how in the days after September 11, she felt as a typical single woman about her sense of not belonging. Some excerpts illustrate this quite well:

> "As I read these heartbreaking reports, I couldn't help but wonder: *Who would I have called*? My dad, who shares coffee with me almost every Friday morning at a mid-town diner? Or my mother, the member of my immediate family most reachable by phone at any given hour? Or perhaps my sister, my best friend since childhood and my truest confidant today? I am not sure.
>
> And that's the point. There is no *one* person whose name would (and should) rise to the top of my list. It's not that there isn't any one; it's that there is no *one* in particular."[2]

The fact that there is no ONE particular person to call does not mean that we do not belong. The single woman *does* have a place. She belongs, first to God, and then to the rich network of relationships that God has prepared for her at home, in her church and at her work place.

Intimacy

As with her sense of belonging, the never married may also feel that being unmarried means that she is deprived of intimacy, something which we all need in life. Thena Ayres contrasts the Western world's perspective of intimacy and the biblical view in a very helpful way.[3]

"Western culture assumes marriage and sexuality as the prime context of intimacy, whereas Scripture assumes and exemplifies a much larger context. Modern approaches have understood human beings biologically, with the sexual drive as one of the dominant motivational forces. A biblical view understands human beings as created for intimacy with God and with one another. Marriage is often a significant framework for the outworking of intimacy, but it is not the only framework."

The restlessness with which many unmarried women pursue intimacy with men outside marriage yields only frustration and disillusionment in the long haul, for true intimacy is found only in a restful posture with God and also with one another. Outside marriage, the primary expression of intimacy can never be sexual union, as that kind of intimacy can only be properly enjoyed within the safe confines of marriage, where one man and one woman give themselves to each other totally and exclusively in relationship.

Sexuality

What, then, is the single woman to do with her life? Is she meant to live an asexual existence? Joseph John makes a helpful distinction between what he calls 'genital sexuality' and 'affective sexuality'. Let me quote from four of his power point slides that he used in a talk entitled 'One is a Whole Number':

1) Single Living is Not an Asexual Existence.

Being single does not mean I leave my 'sexuality' in 'cold storage', that my sexuality is not permitted expression in any way. While genital sexuality is clearly out of bounds for the unmarried, 'affective' sexuality is in no way similarly circumscribed. We are free to be truly sexual here!

2) What is Affectivity or Affective Sexuality?

It is the social dimensions of who we are as sexual beings. It finds expression in acts of affection, compassion, warmth and tenderness. All these are rooted in sexuality although not specifically genital in character. Affective sexuality includes the whole area of our emotional warmth as human beings.

3) What is Genital Sexuality?

Genital sexuality pertains to the biological, physiological, physical and procreative dimension(s) of sexuality. It makes possible the quality of sexual arousal and finds its (highest) expression in the physical act of intercourse. This is reserved for a relationship in which a man and a woman have pledged 'troth' to each other in marriage.

4) The Challenge for the Christian

It is important to realise that there is no fine line that differentiates affective sexuality from genital sexuality. Herein lies the challenge we have as Christians to unashamedly employ our sexuality in ways that will affirm both our lives and the lives of others. Our definitions of intimacy must begin with friendship, not with marriage, as their paradigm. Christ calls all of us in friendship (cf. John 15:14). Our thinking about closeness and touch should be culturally appropriate and contemporary embodiments of such biblical injunctions as in Romans 16:16 (greet one another with a holy kiss), John 13:14 (you ought to wash one another's feet), and John 15:17 (to love one another).

Waiting

Life is all about waiting. We spend years waiting to grow up, weeks waiting for examination results, months waiting to get that first job, and what seems like eternity waiting for a promotion. Yet many unmarried women find that 'waiting' to get married is both unwelcome and challenging.

What Does the Bible Teach about Waiting?

The prophet Isaiah (40:28-31, NKJV) declares that "those who wait on the Lord shall renew their strength." Instead of becoming weary, faint, and exhausted through waiting, we become energised when we wait on the Lord.

Psalm 27:13-14 highlights the importance of waiting for God to act. In Psalm 127, we are warned not to take things into our own hands:

God has a purpose for your life. He may want you to be married or He may want you to be single. If His purpose is that you should remain single, for whatever period of time, then whatever plans you make for finding a life partner, whether through dating agencies or through your own social networks, will amount to nothing. You might find someone, but if it is not of the Lord, the marriage that you build together will collapse. On the other hand, if you trust God to watch over your city of singleness, you do not need to spend sleepless nights, filling your mind with anxious thoughts. He will watch over you better than any watchman.

Are You Waiting to Get Married?

Two of the most dreaded questions for some unmarried women are "Are you alone?" and "Are you waiting for someone?"[4] The answer to the first question is obvious enough. If you are alone, you are alone. It is hard to pretend that you are not. However, the answer to the second question is not so easy to answer honestly.

The desire to get married may be muted or postponed for a whole host of reasons. Societal norms in many countries in Asia may make it difficult for a single woman to admit to others that she is still waiting to get married, especially if she is no longer young.

Some women decide, fairly early in life, that they will remain single. But others are still waiting to get married, even though they are well past the age of child-bearing.

Who are You Waiting for?

If your answer to the former question "Are you waiting to get married?" is "yes" or "maybe", you then need to clarify who you are waiting for. If you wait indefinitely, without a clear sense of what that person should look like (physically, emotionally and spiritually), you may not even recognise him when God brings him into your life. If you do not have any idea of who you are waiting for and the waiting becomes prolonged, your anxiety may become unmanageable.

What Should Your Attitude be While Waiting?

Be patient while you wait for God's plan to be worked out in your life.

> "Be patient with your singleness. He knows the biological clock is ticking. He understands your deepest desires for a spouse. Ask God to give you His perspective on time. You need to develop the kind of endurance that marathon runners have. Mile after mile they plod along, focusing their minds on the unseen finish line. Allow the Holy Spirit to strengthen your endurance. Hope in God will carry you through the long nights and frustrating days."[5]

Continue to trust God while you wait. Psalm 37:3-4 reminds us that if we delight ourselves in the Lord, He will give us the desires of our heart. The question is not whether our desire to get married is right or wrong but whether we can commit our singleness to Him and allow Him to give us what is best for us.

Remind yourself daily that God is good. Marriage is only one possible proof of His goodness to us. It is not the only proof. Many unmarried women can testify that God shows His goodness to them by keeping them single.

At the same time, remind yourself that God is loving. Do not believe the lie that many unmarried women believe – God loves those who get married but has either forgotten the unmarried, or that God loves them less by making them wait for a life partner or even by keeping them single for life. It is a good idea to journal every evidence of God's love in your life so that you do not get deceived into believing that God loves you less than your married sisters.

Acknowledge God as the reigning monarch of your life each day, and that He knows what is best for you – marriage or singleness. Speculation about whether you will ever marry as the years go by is futile as it only creates anxiety. Live one day at a time in the shadow of His wings and enjoy it! After all, God's ways are higher than our ways and His thoughts are higher than our thoughts.

Never allow negative feelings about your unmarried state to linger in your heart and mind. Instead, as Paul exhorts – "whatever is true, whatever is noble, whatever is right, whatever is pure, whatever is lovely, whatever is admirable – if anything is excellent or praiseworthy, think about such things. Whatever you have learned or received or heard from me, or see in me – put it into practice. And the God of peace will be with you" (Philippians 4:8-9).

Loneliness

"Loneliness, which usually refers to a lack of companionship and fellowship, is part of every human life, not just that of the single person. Loneliness may well accompany special missions, moments of decision, bereavement, betrayal, separation from the community of faith, and misfortune."[6]

The unmarried woman will often be alone. But she need never feel lonely. Jesus experienced aloneness when He was tempted in the wilderness: "He was with the wild animals, and angels attended Him" but He had no human companionship. (Mark 1:13). He was sometimes alone when He travelled (Matthew 8:19, 20), and He was certainly alone when His disciples deserted him at the time of his arrest (Mark 14:50). But

He was not lonely because He was always in close communion with God the Father. Only once was He lonely – when on the Cross He was made sin for us and cried out, "My God, my God, why have you forsaken me?" (Matthew 27:46).

While the unmarried woman need never feel lonely, it is unfortunately the case that loneliness often arises from broken relationships. Central to God's purpose for His people are relationships with Him and with others. "Our fellowship is with the Father and with His Son, Jesus Christ ...if we walk in the light, as he is in the light, we have fellowship with one another..." (1 John 1:3, 7). When loneliness is the result of broken relationships either with God or with others, the relationships need to be mended before the loneliness can be got rid of. Just filling our lives with activities to escape from loneliness may work to some extent in our younger days but it certainly does not help us face times when we have no choice but to be alone.

In fact, in order to have an intimate relationship with Christ, we must withdraw periodically from human companionship in order to meet with Him. Such aloneness with Christ is desirable and quite different from the pain of loneliness. We are never truly alone because of our friend, Jesus (Proverbs 18:24; John 15:15). Unmarried women can enjoy these periods of time alone with God much longer and more frequently than a married woman who has to attend to the needs of her husband and children.

ACCEPTING YOUR SITUATION AS A SINGLE

Some women, especially those with successful careers and happy relationships with their extended families, are quite happy to accept their single state. However, there are many who do not find it so easy. So long as their careers take priority in their lives, they may not be thinking too much about the implications of remaining single for a long period of their lives. Below are some case studies of the never-married who have learned to accept their singleness at different periods of their lives.

From Running after a Potential Husband to Running after God

Shirley never imagined that she would stay single for very long. Like almost every other single Christian woman, she had spent most of her twenties praying fervently for a husband. She took every opportunity to try to meet her future husband. She relentlessly hunted down men, but they seemed to escape from her almost as fast as they were caught. She was just unable to maintain a good relationship for any length of time.

The years slipped by. Finally, her dreaded 30th birthday arrived and she was still unattached. By then she was a nervous wreck, feeling like a total failure despite her achievements in sports and her good looks. A close friend of hers suggested to her that, perhaps instead of running after men, she should run after God. She should get to know God better and build a strong relationship with Him first. Shirley was persuaded and God put a new hunger in her heart for Him. She began to trust Him to make 'all things beautiful in His time'. She began to enjoy her singleness. She no longer looked at single men as potential husbands but began to enjoy relating to them as their younger or older sister.

From Waiting in a Long Queue to Sharing the Good News of the Gospel

Yumiko had prayed for years for a life partner. As a Japanese woman, from a very traditional Japanese family, she knew in her heart that when she became a Christian, she was giving up her chances of marriage.

Yumiko was in her mid-thirties when she became a Christian. God gave her so much joy as she learned to follow Jesus. Before Yumiko became a Christian, just seeing a happy family with children would make her heart ache. "Will my turn ever come? Will I ever get married? Will I ever have children of my own?"

Today, she is a changed person. She has completely dedicated her life to share the good news of the gospel of Jesus Christ. God has given her the gift of evangelism and she has led many of her colleagues to Christ. Most of them are single women like her. They are all completely open to marriage but in the meantime, they 'seek first the kingdom of God and His righteousness' (Matthew 6:33) and trust Him for their future, whether they would get married at some stage or remain single for life.

From Self-pity to Care and Concern for Others

Leticia, a Filipina, decided on her 50th birthday that enough was enough. She had been longing and waiting for a husband to show up. Someone had prophesied over her that she would be married by the time she was 45 but nothing happened. She had plunged into depression on her 45th birthday as she thought that either the 'prophetess' was wrong or she herself must be so undesirable that even God could not help her find a husband.

Her church family lovingly nursed her back to spiritual health. They encouraged her to seek the Lord about her future. After extended prayer and consultation with her pastors, she decided to go to the mission field. God was faithful. He helped her with all the cross-cultural adjustments so much that after the first six months, she was sometimes mistaken for a local. She found where she belonged because she surrendered her singleness to God. She is still open to marriage but she no longer wallows in self-pity because she is unmarried. Indeed, God has made all things beautiful in His time!

From Grumbling to Grace

60-year-old Margaret looked more like 70. As the eldest sibling in a family of ten, life had been tough for her. Although she was a mature Christian and had effectively mentored many younger people, she was always grumbling. There was always something wrong with other people. She did not realise that all this incessant grumbling was actually a projection of her resentment and anger with God because she had missed her 'marriage boat'.

Margaret retired at 60 to take care of her mother. But she was now able to spend more time on prayer. She even went away for quiet retreats. On one of these retreats, God spoke to her through these words of Scripture. "My grace is sufficient for you, for my power is made perfect in weakness" (2 Corinthians 12:9). She was so moved by these words that she promised

God that from then on, she would no longer grumble so much but learn to live by grace. God has so transformed her that her frowns and knitted eyebrows have been replaced by the joy on her face and the twinkle in her eye.

DEALING WITH TROUBLESOME EMOTIONS

The emotions discussed below are not exclusive to singles. Married people have to face these too but whereas married couples work through the emotions together as a couple, the single woman needs to walk through this journey on her own as it may be singularly unhelpful to talk to the one she is envious of, discouraged or angry with.

Dealing with Envy

Clayton, in her excellent book *Victory in Singleness*, unpacks the meaning of envy very skilfully for the unmarried woman. She explains that envy is often the result of unfulfilled dreams and the result of being trapped in thinking that God is ignoring her, or that God is unfair because she is still single and others are married.

Clayton defines envy as "the unpleasant feeling of wanting what another person has and feeling bad you don't have it." [7] The unmarried woman may find herself envying another woman who has a husband and children, and feels resentful that she does not have such a 'family'.

Proverbs 14:30 gives a vivid picture of what envy does to us. "A heart at peace gives life to the body, but envy rots the bones." Envy is a deadly emotion and should never be granted even squatters' rights in the life of a single woman.

In order to be set free from envy, Clayton suggests that we need to free ourselves from two types of trapped thinking. The first is that God is ignoring us. The second is that God is unfair. We know that we are in the first trap if we find ourselves saying these things about God:

- He is neglecting me!

- Where is God in my life?
- He doesn't love me because He hasn't answered my prayer.
- Others are more important to Him.
- He's never around when I need Him.[8]

Clayton then goes on to suggest that:

> "To free yourself from the belief that God is ignoring you and eliminate the bondage that those feelings are sure to produce, you must replace them with three truths that must be permanently deposited in your heart:
>
> - Truth #1: God has a plan for your life (Jeremiah 29:11).
> - Truth #2: He will never leave you nor forsake you (Hebrews 13:5).
> - Truth #3: God causes all things to work out for your good (Romans 8:28)."[9]

As for the second trapped thinking that says that "God is unfair", we generally mean that God treats us less favourably than we deserve. Clayton states that we must understand God's perspective of the word 'unfair'.

> "God's definition of the word 'unfair' is grace. Grace means that we receive more patience from God than we deserve. It means there is no limit to the number of times He forgives us. It says that He will love all of us, even the parts that don't deserve to be loved. God is full of grace, and He never runs out (1 Timothy 1:14). Therefore grace is the promise (or agreement) that God makes with Himself that He will treat us unfairly – that He will give us more than we really deserve. If God were fair, we would receive punishment, a life without Him, and eternal death. Aren't you glad that God is unfair?"[10]

Dealing with Discouragement

Kate McVeigh, in her book entitled *Single and Loving It! Living Life to the Fullest* devotes a chapter to discouragement. This is what she says about how discouragement affects the single woman. "Discouragement comes knocking on everybody's door at one time or another, and it seems as if that's especially true of singles. But don't be discouraged: God has not forgotten you! The Bible tells us that He's always working on His plan for your life."[11]

Here are three good reasons why singles do not need to be discouraged by their singleness:

1. God has begun a good work in us and He will complete it (Philippians 1:6).
2. God is faithful (1 Thessalonians 5:24).
3. All things work together for good to them that love God (Romans 8:28).

How do we avoid discouragement?

1. We need to realise that discouragement never comes from God. If we are feeling discouraged, we can be sure it is not because God wants us to feel that way.
2. We need to make God our source. We must always remember that true joy comes from God alone and not from being married (Psalm 27:1).
3. Rejoice with the blessings of others. "Rejoice with those who rejoice; and mourn with those who mourn" (Romans 12:15).
4. Resist the devil when you are tempted to be discouraged, and he will flee from you (James 4:7).
5. Take delight in the Lord; and He will give you the desires of your heart (Psalm 37:4).
6. Don't put everything on hold until you get married. Get on with life. This is the best antidote for discouragement. Know what your life

goals are – what God has called you to do. Buy a house, learn life skills such as cooking, how to change light bulbs, what to do in a car accident, how to manage your finances, and all the things that you wish a husband could do for you.

MAKING ALL THINGS BEAUTIFUL IN THE NEVER-MARRIED

The book of Proverbs which contains some of the most profound sayings about the world has this to say of beauty. "Charm is deceptive, and beauty is fleeting; but a woman who fears the Lord is to be praised" (Proverbs 31:30).

As single women go through life, however, this key biblical teaching can sometimes seem so unreal, unattractive and unattainable to them for various reasons. They may have to wait a long time, even indefinitely, for their much-longed-for life partner to show up in their lives. Others may have been hurt through broken relationships which they hoped would lead to marriage.

How can such women still believe that God makes their singleness beautiful?

The never married can indeed walk through the discomfort, heartache and suffering experienced by them during the single season of their life. To be single and remain grateful to God, contented, even excited about our opportunities to live a full life – that is not just a beautiful dream, but a beautiful reality if we follow God's design for our lives.

CONCLUSION

What makes a woman beautiful is not her good looks, good thoughts or even good deeds. True beauty is a reflection of Christ who is the embodiment of grace and truth. He gives us not what we deserve, but much more than we deserve.

Let us not get stuck in the rut of singleness. If a wheel of a car is stuck in deep mud, the more we rev the engine, the deeper it will be stuck. It is the same with those who feel stuck in the rut of singleness. The more we struggle to get out of singleness, the more 'trapped' we will feel. What is needed is for someone strong enough to come alongside us and lift the car above the muddy groove so that it can run again. In the same way, let God, who loves you deeply and unconditionally, whatever your past looks like, lift you out of your rut of singleness.

Let gratitude be the keynote of our lives. Instead of day-dreaming and continuing to fantasise about romance, allow God's grace to overflow into and out of our lives for that is the essence of beauty which will not fade with time. Whether that Prince Charming ever comes into our lives or not, we know that we already have the Prince of Peace who has promised never to leave us nor forsake us.

6

Reasons for Singleness

Every woman who is single, either by choice or circumstance, can give a variety of reasons for her singleness. Some of these reasons may be genuine ones which may also explain why she is happy or unhappy about her singleness. Other reasons, however, may stem from distorted views of love and marriage, unreal expectations of the perfect life partner, or unresolved fears that she may not even be aware of.

This chapter will explore these reasons, especially in the context of Asian families. The purpose of doing this is to enable the single woman to see that some of the reasons are poor reasons for wanting to remain single. However, there may be other reasons which are truly God-centred and the result of surrender to His sovereign purpose, even though the process of getting to this point of surrender may be a long and difficult one.

The reasons given by single women to explain why they remain single through life may be grouped as follows:

- No desire
- No time
- No opportunities

NO DESIRE FOR MARRIAGE

Some women just do not sense the need for marriage, at least when they are still in their twenties. Life is full enough for them and they have no desire for marriage. They may want to have boyfriends, a serious relationship, or even a baby just for the experience, but marriage is far from their thoughts! What are the contributing factors to this lack of desire for marriage?

Individualism

Women who are well educated, highly qualified, able to buy their own home, and enjoy both their career and social life may well ask, "What's in this marriage business for me?" They consider that they already have a good life and are reluctant to give it up for the sake of marriage.

Increasingly, the rise of individualism, the desire for independence, freedom and flexibility are becoming the predominant reasons why many single women today show no interest in marriage.

Even if the benefits of singleness outweigh those of marriage, is it right for a Christian woman to have no desire for marriage for purely selfish reasons? There may be some who are so clear that God has called them to singleness from a very young age that they have never had any thoughts of marriage. I know of one such person who has since gone home to be with the Lord. She really had the gift of singleness for she had never been interested in any man as a potential life partner, nor had any man tried to date her.

However, among the large number of single women whom I know personally, most have admitted that they have always had the desire to be married but that desire was just never fulfilled. The desire to get married is not wrong and is perfectly normal. It is what we do with the desire that determines whether we are fulfilling God's purpose for our life or whether we are going our own way.

Many women who claim to have no desire for marriage actually dearly wish to be married but are too embarrassed or ashamed to admit it. This embarrassment or shame may arise because of two situations which are difficult for some single Christian women to handle. The first is the nature of Asian society which still tends to expect everyone to get married. The second is the fact that some churches focus all their activities on families, leaving singles on the fringe.

For those who really lack the desire for marriage, what are some real reasons for this lack of desire?

Distorted Views of Marriage

Some have no desire for marriage because they have distorted views of marriage. Most of these views may have been passed down from parents, while some may have been formed from their own observations of marriages that have turned sour or ended in divorce. However, for many single women living in Asia today, the greatest influence on their views about singleness comes from the media, especially the Internet. Both these sources – family of origin and the media – help to shape the single woman's thinking about singleness and marriage.

Marriage is Full of Difficulties

Parents who struggle in their own marriage are the most convincing examples to their children that marriage is full of difficulties and not to be sought after, unless one has no choice. These struggles may be financial in nature, for example, when parents are always squabbling over money matters.

Another example may be about how to bring up the children. For example, when a wife goes back to her parents' home with her children every time her husband disagrees with the way that she handles the children, she is only confusing them about the respective roles of the parents in their lives. She is also sending out a signal that she is more capable, together with her parents, of bringing up the children instead of their father who may be too harsh, too absent or whatever her own contention may be with her husband. This undoubtedly shapes the children's thinking about marriage when they grow up. They are left feeling very uneasy about how to be loyal to both parents.

When the children grow up, they will also think that their mother and grandparents are great but that the father does nothing apart from bringing home money! It is a tragedy in a marriage when children become the parents' battlefield, and not the object of their love, for they grow up thinking that married life is just too tough for them.

These and many other marital problems have often put such fear and disgust in the hearts of some single women that they have no appetite for marriage. While their desire for intimacy may still be directed to a 'partner', or several 'partners' over a period of time, some have opted for various alternative lifestyles instead of one permanent opposite-sex partner.

Alternative Lifestyles Instead of Marriage

Increasingly, in the more affluent parts of Asia, some single women choose to practise alternative lifestyles instead of entering into a permanent, monogamous relationship with a husband. These lifestyles may take various forms. Some choose co-habitation where a couple lives together as if they were husband and wife but have no intention of ever getting married to each other. Others opt for 'trial' marriages in which a couple lives together for a certain period of time first to see if things would work out for them before they plunge into marriage. Yet other women opt for a lifelong or temporary sexual relationship with other women.

These alternative lifestyles debase the high view of marriage which, as stated in the Bible, is one of God's most sacred gifts to human beings. Women who practise such lifestyles often come from dysfunctional homes, have never experienced love, or have bought into the many lies sold by the media that the desire for intimacy is fulfilled only by sex which does not have to be confined to the marriage bed.

All that needs to be said at this point in our discussion is that God loves women who practise such lifestyles as much as those who follow the biblical way of marriage. But His heart bleeds for those who live in these ways. Like the Samaritan woman at the well in John's Gospel Chapter 4, they seek fulfilment from all the wrong people, and inflict pain and misery on themselves. In order to avoid gossip and disapproving looks, the Samaritan woman drew water from the well only at high noon when no one else was likely to go as it was too hot to go out then.

Times have changed. Today, so many women live the same kind of lifestyle as the Samaritan woman but they do so quite blatantly and are in fact insisting on their right to live this way. It is quite clear from John Chapter 4 that Jesus' heart went out to this woman. He felt sorry for her. He wanted her to find the fulfilment she had been looking for everywhere but which had obviously escaped her. It was when the Samaritan woman honestly admitted that she really had no husband (even though she had five husbands and was then living with someone who was not her husband) and turned to Jesus, believing that He was the Messiah who had come to quench her thirst forever, that she found what she had been looking for all along. She was so excited about finding Jesus that she told everyone in the village that here was someone she wanted them to meet because he had told her everything she ever did.

Unresolved Fears

We may not be aware that the choice to remain single might be based on unresolved fears. For example, a woman may be single because of disappointments, unhealed hurts, a pattern of failed relationships in the past, hidden fears of intimacy, a fear of loss of independence, or unreal expectations about romantic love, marriage and the perfect life partner.

In dealing with fears of intimacy, Purnell highlights the fear of rejection, the fear of losing control (the fear of identity being submerged in a relationship with a man), the fear of facing one's loveless life and self absorption which is destructive fear.[1]

The Kanes, in their excellent book entitled *From Fear to Love*,[2] demonstrate how we can all make new and different choices to move away from our fears and learn to love others – and ourselves – in more healthy and productive ways.

The key chapter in the book that relates directly to our current discussion is Chapter 6. In this chapter, the Kanes deal with three other fears besides the fear of rejection. These are the fear of failure (which arises from perfectionism and from looking at success as good luck), the fear of abandonment (which is accompanied by feeling empty or suspicious and emotional hibernation), and the fear of death (which is characterised by an emotional overload that overwhelms, and the fear of dying physically which is the ultimate finality). The Kanes detail the signs that accompany each type of fear. These signs are very useful for self-diagnosis.

The Kanes also have a very useful chapter (Chapter 7) in which they outline practical steps to overcome our fears. These are summarised as follows:

1. Learn to be a risk-taker
    a) Learn from setbacks
    b) Learn to try again
    c) Learn to be real
2. Develop supportive relationships
    a) Someone to cheer us on, e.g. a coach who will say to us, "It's ok, you can make it."
    b) Words that affirm
3. Make a commitment to growth and change
4. Grow in faith by developing an eternal perspective

NO TIME FOR MARRIAGE

Some single women regret that they did not make time in their younger days to develop relationships that could have led to marriage. There are at least four main areas in a single woman's life which can 'compete' with making time for marriage.

Challenges of a Career

The 21st century woman living in Asia has sufficient education, resources and opportunities to carve out a good career for herself. Where marriage and motherhood are not upheld as a high goal in life for a woman, it is easy to see why a single woman will put her career as her primary goal in life. After all, she can do really well, earn good money and live very comfortably.

However, the challenges that she faces in the process of climbing up the career ladder make her less marriageable, given the fact that most Asian men prefer to marry women who are further 'down' the career ladder. These challenges also leave her no time to socialise with men whom she might want to marry. If she is a Christian, she would look for a man who shares the same values and not be 'unequally yoked' with unbelievers. However, it is a hard fact of life that most of her work colleagues may either be already married or are not Christians, thereby leaving her few or no opportunities of marriage if she spends most of her time at her workplace.

Many Christian single women look to their churches to help them find husbands. But as most of our churches are either completely oblivious of the struggles faced by single women, or are too busy with family-oriented activities that they have neither the time nor the energy to care for singles, the result is that single women, hoping to marry Christian men, end up even more disappointed.

Church Activities

Many marriageable, young Christian women devote whatever time is left over from their careers to some activity or other in church. However, the activities that women are typically involved in are those which men generally shy away from. For example, many single women end up teaching Sunday schools or junior church, or singing in the choir. These are also typically the areas of ministry where there is a great shortage of men. So the chances of a woman meeting Mr Right through these activities are minimal, although some good marriages have undoubtedly been made possible from participation in these same activities.

I am not suggesting that the single woman should join church activities for the purpose of finding a life partner. Nor am I saying that single women should blame their church for their singleness. I am simply pointing out a fact that participation in such activities can be so demanding and time-consuming that it leaves the single woman with no time for much else besides work. In that sense, the church activities leave her no time for building up relationships that could lead to marriage.

Fitness Frenzy

The media is constantly bombarding us with images of women who are not only beautiful but also smart, career-savvy and fit. The desire to keep fit is a wholesome one but it can easily become an idol when the amount of money, time and energy spent on fitness programmes leaves the single woman with no money, time or energy for God!

The single woman living in 21st century Asia is undoubtedly much influenced by what the media presents as 'desirable'. A very high percentage of Korean women have undergone plastic surgery for the sole purpose of looking good. Fitness centres are set up, complete with personal trainers, to lure the unsuspecting single woman to sign up for fitness programmes, which not only drain a large percentage of her income but also her time.

The single woman might persuade herself that she feels good and keeps fit as a result of these programmes. She thus concludes that it is worth the time and money invested. However, there is no known correlation between fitness and the chances of getting married. While a woman may look for fitness in a potential husband, at least one who can live long enough to father any children she may have with him (if they were to get married) and not leave her to be a young widow to raise their children, men are more likely to look for women who will make *them* look and feel good, rather than those who are overly concerned about their own fitness.

NO OPPORTUNITIES FOR MARRIAGE

The woman who fears the Lord and who has dedicated her life to her Saviour and Lord need never fear the lack of opportunities for marriage. God is the divine matchmaker who has an ingenious way of bringing a man and woman together in marriage at the right time.[3] A Christian woman's ultimate goal in life is not to get married. It is to obey her Lord and Master who may have plans for her to be married but who equally may have plans for her to remain single.

Rather than attributing her singleness to a lack of opportunities for marriage, she should trust not in matchmakers and opportunities, but in God who alone knows best whether He can be glorified better through her marriage or her singleness. As the Lord Jesus said to Saul who was persecuting the Christians, He may be saying to those of His daughters who are blaming the lack of opportunities for their singleness, "Why are you persecuting Me? Why are you blaming your church, your parents, your matchmaking agencies and yourself for your perceived lack of opportunities? It hurts *you* to kick against the goads."

Singleness as a Choice

In the preceding sections of this chapter, we have shown how some reasons for singleness are poor reasons. However, there is ONE good reason. Some women have deliberately chosen a single life not out of selfishness but because they have opted to focus time and energy on a challenging career as a way of bringing glory to God rather than to fulfil their own selfish desires.

Others, observing those who unreflectively marry because somehow it is 'the thing to do' decide to make a different choice. They refuse to marry for the wrong reasons. Such wrong reasons would include the need to overcome loneliness, the need for sex, the need for love and intimacy and the need to experience motherhood. All these are real needs but marriage may not be God's way for you to meet your needs. Let it be said, and may it be understood, not only by single women but also by pastors, counsellors, care givers and family members, that blessed are those who, after seeking the Lord's will for their lives, are able to say, "Thank you Lord for keeping me single. I will rejoice in my singleness because I know that is Your perfect plan for me. And I wouldn't want any man to spoil that plan!"

Special honour should be given to those who, although committed to a covenant community of faith, remain single. Some, by choosing to go overseas as missionaries, may circumstantially be eliminating marriage as an option. Many mission agencies and churches fail to realise the immensity of the sacrifice made by such women.

A Loving Appeal to Married Couples

Those who are happily married have a major part that they can play in supporting the 'right' reasons for singleness. Instead of forever trying, naively, to match-make single women against their wishes (and often God's as well) and to their constant embarrassment, they can journey with the single women who may be struggling with their singleness but who deeply desire to walk according to God's will. They can also be the ones to help them get rid of two nagging fears, "Is there something wrong with me?" and "Has God made a mistake?" God promises to set the lonely in families and this will indeed happen if married people could affirm that the single woman is in no way inferior to her married sisters and that God does not love her less because she has not found a husband. They can go a step further by giving her a place of honour for her obedience to God.

CONCLUSION

Many and varied are the reasons as to why some Asian women stay single.

Every single woman reading this book would do well to examine herself to see if her reasons for remaining single are good or poor ones. A self-centred 'what's in it for me' attitude towards marriage, a misplaced identity, a poor self-image, and distorted views of marriage can be corrected in the light of the biblical perspective. Unresolved fears can be released to God in exchange for faith in an everlasting and ever-loving God. When the wrong reasons for remaining single are eliminated, marriage often becomes a real possibility for the single woman who had earlier given up any hopes of marriage!

At the same time, the single woman should also examine the reasons why she wants to be married. There was a time, not so long ago, when it was considered shameful for a woman to admit that she desired to be married.

Today this is no longer the case, even in Asia. The woman who desires marriage should be open to help. She should start praying for her future husband and ask her friends to join her in this prayer. While a woman may intuitively feel the need to play hard to get in order to be sure that her man is really interested in her, some men either dislike such pretence or simply do not understand the signal correctly – that she is interested in him but he must initiate and continue the chase. The result is that far too many women have regretted playing hard to get. By threatening to break off a relationship whenever they did not get their own way, some have regretfully lost boyfriends and fiancés who grew weary of chasing them. By sending out mixed signals, they have lived to regret that they were not truthful either to themselves or to their prospective husbands.

7

Network of Connections

The key to healthy connections is to view restrictions (the things that the single woman cannot enjoy because she is unmarried) not as barriers to happiness but as boundaries lovingly put in place by the Divine Creator and Potter who skilfully moulds each life in its own unique way so as to reflect His glory. Of course this can only happen if we let Him hold the master key to unlock every room in our lives, whether they are reasonably clean or in a real mess.

THE MEANING OF CONNECTEDNESS

In today's world, we seem to be connecting more and more with one another. We can feel connected to all our friends, acquaintances and even complete strangers through such social networks as Facebook and Twitter. We can chat with another person halfway round the world through Skype. We can send text messages and emails, and receive responses almost immediately. Never before in the history of humankind have we been able to stay so well connected. But are we really connecting with one another better? Or are we merely connecting in a disconnected way?

While speed seems so important in our postmodern world, relationships take time to build. Instant relationships which lead to instant marriages only lead to instant breakdowns. Nor is the sheer volume of emails in our inboxes an indication of how well we are connected, especially when the emails do not even get read. Are we compromising the quality of our relationships by replacing it with the quantity of superficial connections?

In an article with the rather provocative title 'Is it too late to unplug the iPod?', the author makes some very perceptive comments about our relationships. "Plugging into iPods and texting incessantly on mobile devices are giving (us) a sense of being connected. In reality, such an activity boxes (us) into social isolation. We have lost the art of oral tradition. We have forgotten the intimacy of real time relating."[1]

THE BIBLICAL PERSPECTIVE OF CONNECTEDNESS

As we understand the nature of our fragmented relationships all competing with one another so desperately for time and attention, let us unplug our iPods and listen afresh to God's way of how we can stay connected to Him and to one another in the intimacy of real time relating.

We all feel the need to stay connected with one another as the world has become a global village. But many strive so hard at making these connections work, only to fail again and again. Why? We cannot really make connections work. We are more than just the sum total of our genes. We cannot be digitalised and made accessible at the click of a mouse in such a way that we instantly become relational beings or are instantly made desirable for relationships. We are made in the image of God who has put in us the capacity to love and to be loved. The concept of love itself has been badly tarnished in today's world and we need to return to the Bible to learn what God, the Author of love, has to say about how to stay connected through love.

The biblical perspective of connectedness is perhaps best summed up in Jesus' final discourse with His disciples before He made His final journey to Jerusalem to die for the sins of the whole world. "I am the vine; you are the branches. If a man remains in me and I in him, he will bear much fruit; apart from me you can do nothing ... If you obey my commands, you will remain in my love, just as I have obeyed my Father's commands and remain in his love. I have told you this so, that my joy may be in you, and that your joy may be complete" (John 15:5, 10, 11).

According to Jesus, the secret to all connectedness is to be connected to God Himself. Just as a branch has no life when cut off from the main tree, it is impossible for us to even think of meaningful connectedness with people in our lives without first being connected to God. What is required is a permanent connectedness to Him. A branch can never afford to take a break from the tree for it would die. In the same way, the key to building healthy relationships with other people is first to build a healthy relationship with God by remaining in His love.

In answering a trick question by a Jewish lawyer about which is the greatest commandment, Jesus said that the first and greatest commandment is "You shall love the Lord your God with all your heart and with all your mind and with all your strength." The second commandment is like the first, "You shall love your neighbour as yourself." Jesus, in answering the question, diverted attention from ourselves first to God and second to others. Herein lies the key to real connectedness – love for God and love for our neighbour.

In championing our rights as postmodern women, we have often forgotten our responsibilities – to God and to the people He has brought into our lives. What is even worse is that in fighting for equality with men, we have become so focused on ourselves and our achievements that we have lost the real secret to a joyful life. It is not, as the world would have us believe, 'me first, me second, and me again'. Joy, so appropriately spelled JOY comes from putting Jesus first, others second and yourself last. This is an important principle which is evident in the numerous case studies of single women reported throughout this book.

IMPORTANCE OF INTERCONNECTEDNESS

In a classic article on singleness, Thena Ayres illustrates the importance of connectedness for the single woman. "It could be said that there is no such thing as singleness. We all live out the joys and sorrows of our lives within a rich complexity of relationships. This is God's intention for all human beings."[2]

There are many reasons why the rich complexity of relationships is so important for the single woman. But we will focus on just four for special mention here. These will again be illustrated with case studies. But instead of sharing other women's case studies, this is an appropriate place to share my own story, for the simple reason that I know it better than any other story and it illustrates well the importance of staying connected.

Support Group

First, the single woman, unlike her married sisters, does not have a natural support group. A woman who is married would naturally turn to her husband and grown-up children for support. The single woman has no husband and children to turn to. But if she would look in the right places and give priority to building good relationships, she would find that God has provided for her a support group to meet her varying needs through the different seasons of life. The single woman may often be troubled by thoughts like "Who can be there for me when I am sick or feeling down or facing a breakup in a relationship?" or "Who will take care of me if I am terminally ill? Or when I am old and unable to take care of myself?"

God has provided a wonderful support group for me through the long decades of my life as a single woman.

There are at least three qualities I look for in a support group. The most important quality is that the members of our support group should really know us and not just be on nodding acquaintance with us. It is often too emotionally tiring and time consuming to have to tell another person all that we are going through, in good times as well as in not-so-good times. If our support group knows us well, they know why we respond in certain ways, where we hurt and what makes us tick.

The second most important quality is that members of our support group should accept us for who we are, warts and all. When I was going through the emotional pain of a breakup in a relationship, a university professor who knew me well gave me the most helpful support. He accepted me for who I was and comforted me very effectively, sometimes with words but more often with actions that showed his heartfelt concern for me. He just seemed to be able to empathise with how I felt. He reassured me, over and over again, that break-ups in relationships happen but that I would find the strength to move on. I did not believe him then and the recovery process took far longer than it should have, but he was right. What he told me often gave me the impetus to work on recovery.

The third important quality I look for in a member of my support group is that he or she should bring out the best in me, and still treat me as a responsible adult even when I make mistakes. When I broke off with my nominally Catholic boyfriend, I was already feeling like a terrible sinner. I felt that I should never have considered marriage with someone who did not have a personal relationship with God. Perhaps it was the loneliness of being a foreign student that blurred my spiritual vision then. Or it may simply have been the fact that we got on so well with each other. However hard I tried to rationalise our relationship, I still felt that I had disobeyed God and deserved to be punished. It was a tremendous relief to me that I did not have to be cross-examined about the reasons for the breakup. What I appreciated most about my professor-friend was that he gave me space to grieve and time to let the wounds heal instead of rubbing salt into them.

As a single woman gets older, or if she becomes seriously ill or less mobile, her support group should include people who can help her with her physical needs. Even routine jobs may become a challenge in infirmity. In 2003 when the SARS epidemic hit Singapore quite drastically, I once had to quarantine myself as I had come down with flu-like symptoms. I was then living on my own but was so thankful to God that He had provided me with a very caring neighbour and other women in my small group who willingly volunteered to bring me food. It turned out to be a false alarm and I was actually well enough to take care of myself and all my household chores. But should I really need physical help, I know there are people whom I can call upon for support.

Accountability

A married woman is expected to be accountable to her husband, and to her children if she has any. A single woman, however, can go through life being accountable to no one except her boss at her workplace. If she is the boss herself, then she may never need to be accountable to anyone except a board of directors who may not know much about how her company is run on a daily basis. She can get away with very little accountability.

At home, a single woman can live entirely for herself but this is not healthy for her. If there is no one in her life to speak the truth to her about her weaknesses and shortcomings, she may well go through life unchanged, unattached and unfulfilled. She may have serious character flaws but may be totally unaware of them unless someone points them out to her. If she knows about the number of people that she has offended by the same character flaw, whether it is her bad temper, her tendency to gossip or something else, she might be more willing to change. Of course, there are those who refuse to change or tell themselves that they are too old to change. They believe that as it was in the beginning, so it is now, and forever will be – whatever her character may be like.

The system of accountability that is set up at her work place may be the only place where the single woman is aware of the need to make herself accountable to someone. If she has to finish a project by a certain deadline, she is expected to complete it in time and excuses will not be readily accepted. Where such systems of accountability exist, the single woman becomes quite good at making herself accountable.

Accountability is important not only in our workplace but in all our relationships. In a world that continues to focus on rights rather than responsibilities, accountability for the single woman is often neglected. After all, since she is single, why can't she just enjoy her freedom and do whatever she pleases? Who does she need to be accountable to? Why is accountability even necessary?

The Bible teaches that "two are better than one;... If one falls, his friend can help him up" (Eccelesiastes 4:9-10). If the single woman falls, either physically, emotionally or spiritually, who is there to help her up? If her heart has grown cold towards God and towards men because of past disappointments, how can she warm herself again unless there is someone willing to come alongside her and light a spark in her life again?

My best accountability partners are also my prayer partners. For many years, I have met up periodically with a few other single women who know me well, love me despite my failings, and are at complete liberty to ask me any awkward question about myself, my hopes and fears, the way I spend my leisure and even my 'thorn in the flesh'. I have never dodged their questions as I know that they ask these questions for my own good and not to gather fuel for gossip. When we pray together, we realise that the ground is level at the foot of the Cross. Nobody is superior to anyone else in any way. We are all dependent on the mercy and grace of Christ to forgive us our sins. We feel we understand each other and our mutual accountability goes a long way.

Catalyst for Growth

While other single women may be the best people to hold us accountable for what we think, say and do in life, they may not be as effective as catalysts for our own spiritual growth. The need to grow in Christ-likeness is not challenged when we are with like-minded people, especially with those whom we share common experiences.

Thus, in order to stay connected with the world at large, the single woman needs to be in touch not only with other single women but also with men and women of different socio-economic backgrounds, cultures and age groups. We may find it much easier to relate to people who are like us, but it is those who are distinctly different from us who provide the biggest catalyst for our own growth. Unfortunately, a lot of single women stop growing after a certain age as they prefer to stay within their own safety zones.

Let me illustrate how connections with people different from us can be a catalyst for our own growth with two case studies from my own life.

First, there is the challenge of how to relate to people from other cultures. Intercultural studies teach us to think that when we find people behaving differently from us because they come from other cultures, we should not immediately think that we are right and they are wrong, or that we are efficient and that they do not know any better. They are just different from us and if we take the trouble to find out why they do certain things their way, we often begin to understand them and ourselves better. I am not talking about spiritual truths which are unchanging, and moral behaviour which should not be compromised. I am talking about ways of doing things for which there is no clear right or wrong.

When I was an undergraduate, my professors were mainly Westerners as I majored in English Literature. They questioned some of my assumptions about what is appropriate classroom behaviour. As we had never been taught to question our teachers in school, I found it extremely difficult to even speak up in class, unless I had a question to ask. Even then, I would prefer to speak to the professor after class instead of exposing myself to the risk of asking a stupid question. Later, when I became a university professor myself, I worked hard to help the students think for themselves instead of just regurgitating everything that they had been taught. This was growth, not only for me, but my students as well. I no longer thought that those who were very vocal were trouble makers as I gave my students permission to disagree with me if I was wrong.

Another area of growth, one that I least expected, was in intergenerational interaction. One of the things I did in my retirement was to nurture a group of young China nationals living in Singapore who had become Christians. They looked up to me as their spiritual mother. But what I did not expect was that they would call me by my first name, feel really at home with me, and even take it upon themselves to point out my weaknesses. I did not like it at first but through them, God taught me many precious lessons. Young people today expect to be treated with respect, which usually means that they are begging for their own private space and to be treated as responsible adults. We need to teach the younger generation to treat our elders with respect but their way of showing respect may be somewhat different from what we expect. We also should not forget that everyone needs to be respected, even children.

It may be more comfortable to stay within our own self-assigned safety zones. But I, for one, am glad that God really used the younger generation from China not only to strengthen my own faith as I dialogued continually with them about God but also that through such interactions, some of the fruit of the Spirit, especially love, gentleness, patience and peace, grew a bit bigger in me.

Staying Relevant to Changing Times

Married women are more or less forced to stay relevant to changing times if they have children. The world is changing so rapidly that we can sometimes despair about whether we can ever stay relevant. But if we consider staying relevant as a major goal in our life, we will make certain wise decisions and reserve some time and energy for ongoing learning.

Most single women today are working women. As systems are overhauled in the light of the latest technology, they too are forced to stay relevant to changing times. But staying relevant is not just about keeping abreast with technology, important as that is.

For the Bible-believing single woman, staying relevant means a number of things. It means understanding people's aspirations today, the books they read, the movies they watch, how they spend their time, their values and so on. It means understanding the heartbeat of this generation but not necessarily agreeing with its values, especially when they are contradictory to Scripture. As the Bible is God's truth for all generations, the single woman must take the time and trouble to read God's Word and sit at the feet of those who continue to see the relevance of the Bible in everyday life and who apply God's truth relevantly in our postmodern world.

CHARACTERISTICS OF HEALTHY RELATIONSHIPS

There are three factors which contribute to healthy relationships.

Seeing Our Relationships from the Right Perspective

First, we need to see our relationships from the right perspective. We need to see all our relationships, provided they are not sinful ones, as God's gift to us for our particular season of life. All our existing relationships have been handpicked by our loving, heavenly Father to teach us how to become more like Jesus. This applies not only to relationships that we have initiated but also and especially to those relationships for which we have no choice – like those in our family of origin, and those which are a constant challenge to us.

Let me illustrate this with one relationship from my own life. When I was acting head of department at a university in Singapore, I often failed to see that the most difficult and contentious colleagues were God's gift to me, sent specially by Him to develop my Christian character. I only saw them as difficult trouble makers robbing me of peace and rest every day. Several years after one such colleague left, we met at a conference and I learnt for the first time, that when he was in Singapore, his marriage had just broken up and he was seeing a psychiatrist every week. When we met again, he had recovered sufficiently to realise how horrible he had been to me and apologised profusely when we met. It was a most unlikely but beautiful reconciliation, one that the good Lord himself initiated. Through this, I learned that people are never to be regarded as a nuisance but as God's gift to us, even though we may not appreciate them all the time.

Seeing the Mutuality of All Relationships

The biggest threat to healthy relationships is what I call the 'you versus me' or 'them versus us' divide. For example, when we see our families not as 'us' but 'you versus me' and when we see our church as 'them versus me', we are not laying the right foundation for good relationships. If we would only change our mindset and our language to the "we-ours-us" paradigm in all our relationships, they have a much better chance of becoming really healthy. We need to take joint ownership of our relationships and be set free from blaming one another when things go wrong.

Developing Our Relationships along Healthy Dimensions

Besides acknowledging that all healthy relationships begin and end with God, and that each relationship is His gift to us, we also need to actively develop our relationships by

- Recognising differences
- Appreciating other people's opinions and ways of doing things
- Putting ourselves in the other person's shoes
- Expressing ourselves truthfully and lovingly (speaking the truth in love)
- Developing oneness and team spirit

Establishing Boundaries in Our Relationships

One of the best resources on how to build healthy relationships is *Boundaries* written by Henry Cloud and John Townsend.[3] They did not set themselves up as 'relationship gurus'. They started out by helping people when to say 'yes', when to say 'no', and how to take control of their lives. They did not try to fix every relational problem. But their godly wisdom and combined experience as counsellors provide a treasure chest full of surprises for those who are determined to build healthy relationships.

One of the most effective ways to develop healthy relationships is to establish boundaries as they affect all areas of our lives:

- Physical boundaries help us determine who may touch us, how and when.
- Mental boundaries give us freedom to have our own thoughts and opinions.
- Emotional boundaries help us deal with our own emotions and disengage us from the harmful, manipulative emotions of others.
- Spiritual boundaries help us distinguish God's will from our own and give us renewed awe for our Creator.

CONCLUSION

In this chapter, we have explained the biblical perspective of connectedness. We have given four main reasons for why interconnectedness is especially important for the single woman – to be a support group, to make her accountable, to act as a catalyst for growth and to help her stay relevant in changing times. We have also touched upon the topic of how to maintain healthy relationships. Of chief concern is the question of how to establish boundaries in all our relationships.

8

Connection with Family of Origin

This chapter deals with the single woman's connection with her family of origin. The focus will be on the relationship between unmarried daughters and their parents, unmarried sisters and their siblings.

UNMARRIED DAUGHTERS AND THEIR PARENTS

Biblical Teaching on Honouring Parents

The Bible teaches very clearly and emphatically the importance of honouring our parents. The first commandment that deals with 'love for neighbour' as distinct from 'love for God' is the fifth commandment which reads as follows, "Honour your father and your mother, so that you may live long in the land the Lord your God is giving you" (Exodus 20:12; Deuteronomy 5:16).

The Meaning and Significance of 'Honouring' Parents

The main meaning of 'honour' is 'to weigh heavily; to be weighty, honoured and enjoy respect.' God expects us to give due weight to what our parents do and say. We are not to make light of them or belittle them in any way, even in their senior years when they no longer seem relevant to the fast-changing, postmodern world we live in. We are to honour and respect them at all times.

Relevance of this Commandment Today

First, we need to be clear in our own minds that the fulfilment of the fifth commandment does not depend on whether parents are worthy of honour. Parents do have duties to their children and if they fail, they are answerable to God. It is, of course, easier for adult unmarried daughters to honour parents who are worthy of honour. But God expects ALL children, young or old, married or single, to honour their parents, regardless of what they are like.

Of course, for an adult, unmarried daughter who is a Christian, there are times when honouring her parents would mean disobedience to God. For example, she would not be able to hold joss sticks anymore, or worship at the ancestral altar because her God has commanded her not to have any other gods besides Him. However, she should continue to show that she is committed to loving and honouring her parents in other ways while they are still alive.

On matters of marriage, the unmarried daughter who has resolved in her mind never to marry an unbeliever so as not to be 'unequally yoked' should not give in to the pressure from her parents to marry an unbeliever. Parents often lower their standards for their daughters as they get older and may be quite glad for them to get married to any man, so long as they get married! In all such situations of genuine conflict, it is good to remember an important principle – love for Jesus must overrule all other loves. "Anyone who loves his father or mother more than Me is not worthy of Me" (Matthew 10:37).

Practical Ways of Honouring Our Parents in Asia Today

The first practical way in which we can honour our parents is to allow them to show their love for us in ways that are appropriate to our age. Our parents do not stop being our parents when we become adults, although their love for us would need to be expressed differently from when we were children.

A second way in which we can honour our parents is to look after them, especially in their old age. Some parents invest their entire life savings in the education of their children. The least that children should do for such parents is to give them enough money to live on when they are too old to work. However, giving money without love is NOT honouring parents. Even as some people give money to a beggar simply to get rid of him, without showing any real concern for his plight, so it is possible to provide for one's parents financially in their old age and yet be unwilling to love them or to care for them in any way.

WHAT PARENTS EXPECT OF THEIR UNMARRIED DAUGHTERS

What Asian parents expect of their unmarried daughters varies from family to family, from one generation to another, and from one country to another. In general, their expectations may be financial, social, psychological or physical.

Financial Expectations

In many parts of Asia, it is quite common for adult children – whether married or not, so long as they are working – to give money to their parents. This custom started because a few decades ago, immigrants to Southeast Asia often left China or India with very little money and earthly possessions. As they also tended to have large families, the older children in a large family often had to help finance the living expenses and even the education of the younger children.

Another reason why Asian parents expect their adult children to give them money on a monthly basis is because they think that it is a practical way for children to show their gratitude and love to their parents.

A third reason, found mostly among the less educated Asian parents, is because they do not have pension funds for their retirement years, or because the funds are not adequate for the escalating standards of living.

These expectations may look perfectly reasonable. But very often they cannot be met for two main reasons: (i) the daughter's own finances are barely adequate for herself and she is not in a position to support her elderly parents; (ii) the daughter is unwilling to contribute towards the finances of the family for a variety of reasons – she may feel less loved by her parents than her siblings, she may still be envious of her siblings being better off financially, she may be the youngest in her family and have got used to her older siblings doing everything for the family.

Social Expectations

Older Asian parents often expect their unmarried daughters to build their social lives around them. This is especially so when the daughters have a single parent. Some unmarried daughters in Asia have no social life of their own. Apart from work commitments, their days and nights are spent completely in the company of their parents and the friends of their parents.

Other parents, anxious for their unmarried daughters to get married, may build their social life around parties or appointments for the daughter to meet eligible young men. Some have indeed found husbands as a result of their mothers' efforts but for every success story, there are probably twice as many stories of unmarried daughters who dearly wish that their mothers would take the pressure off them and allow them space and time to enjoy their friends, without thinking of 'husband hunting' all the time.

Psychological Expectations

Some Asian parents expect their unmarried daughters to give them psychological support. This is especially so when the mother has had to go through trauma like the loss of a husband through death or divorce, or the untimely death of a child. Mother and daughter can grieve together but it is unhealthy for the unmarried daughter if her mother continues to feed her with negative feelings about marriage and 'transfer' to her daughter her own feelings of betrayal, rejection and other such negative feelings.

Physical Expectations

It is common for Asian parents to expect their unmarried daughters to be physically present with them when they are ill, especially when they know that their days are numbered. As most unmarried daughters these days have to work to earn a living, this expectation is difficult to meet. Many, especially those who are financially well off, choose to employ a full-time domestic helper to take care of the physical needs of their elderly parents.

Problems with Parental Expectations

When we consider parental expectations as a part of the relationship between parents and unmarried daughters, there are two common problems that can arise. The first is that of over-protectiveness. Some parents over-protect their unmarried daughters by continuing to cook, clean and do their laundry for them instead of letting them learn to take care of themselves and their parents. Such behaviour is unhealthy for the unmarried daughters because their parents continue to treat them as children rather than as adults. It also does not encourage independence and growth, both of which are particularly important for the single woman.

The second relational problem is over-independence. Some elderly parents value their independence so much that they insist on living on their own even when they are too frail to take care of themselves. Not every unmarried daughter can afford to pay for the services of a live-in domestic helper and when elderly parents keep falling and breaking their bones, or meet with other domestic accidents, they can be a continuous source of tension for the unmarried daughter who may still have to run to their rescue even if she is not staying with them.

WHAT UNMARRIED DAUGHTERS EXPECT OF THEIR PARENTS

Unmarried daughters may be willing to provide money and even get a domestic helper to take care of their parents. But in general, they prefer to run their own lives, involving parents in their decisions only as advisors occasionally. They also do not expect to spend too much time with their parents. If their parents are living with them, they expect them to fall in line with the house rules and may even value their priced belongings, like expensive furniture, and expensive cars much more than their parents' feelings of comfort.

MISMATCH IN EXPECTATIONS

The gap between the expectations of the unmarried daughters and that of their parents is often a big and unhappy one. Not many actively seek to close it. The unmarried daughter may be too caught up in her own career and happiness to even notice her parents' heartache. She provides for them but only financially and does not meet any of her parents' physical, social and psychological expectations. The parents may be too hurt to be able to express their feelings in ways considered acceptable by their unmarried daughter. They may also be too fearful to raise objections about the way that they are treated. As things stand, elderly parents often get shouted at for the slightest thing – for being slow, for keeping everyone waiting, for making a mess when they eat, and so on and so forth.

UNMARRIED SISTERS AND SIBLINGS

In many parts of Asia, it is common for unmarried siblings to live together in the same house. There are some advantages in this arrangement. If they get along well with each other, they can form a family nucleus, support each other emotionally, and share the domestic chores.

However, as with the expectations of unmarried daughters and their parents, there may be a mismatch between what unmarried sisters expect of their siblings, especially those who are married, and what their siblings expect of them.

Three of the most common problems are: (i) sibling rivalry, (ii) relating to the unmarried sisters as if they are still children, and (iii) relating to the married sibling as if his/her spouse does not exist.

Sibling Rivalry

Sibling rivalry is the kind of rivalry found among siblings in large families, especially those who are close in age and in birth order within the family. It occurs when one sibling gets more attention than another or when he/she perceives things that way.

Some types of sibling rivalry die in childhood. Once the siblings grow up, they can look back at their childish behaviour and just laugh together about it. However, many siblings do not realise that some of this sibling rivalry may be quite deep rooted and they may go through life, thinking that "Dad loves my brother more than me" or "Mum thinks that my sister is always right, just because she is the first born and older than me." Some of it may be untrue and merely a matter of perception that "dad or mum is unfair."

For the unmarried sister, such sibling rivalry may spoil her relationship with her siblings especially if the latter are married.

Relating to the Unmarried Sisters as if They are Still Children

Older siblings sometimes continue to treat their unmarried sisters as if they were still children. It is the same problem as parents who do everything for their grown-up unmarried daughters and do not give them enough space to be themselves.

Problems arise when the siblings forget that they have grown up. Unless both have never left home and are very similar in character the chances are that the gap in their thinking, personal preferences, choice of friends and activities to participate in, even choice of favourite foods, may widen as the years go by. Treating an unmarried sibling like a child can result in conflict.

Relating to the Married Sibling as if His/Her Spouse Does Not Exist

Unmarried sisters need to realise that their married siblings, especially their brothers, are not the same siblings they had in their childhood. When they were children, they were free to play together, share, quarrel, to compete, and just to be themselves with each other.

However, once a sibling gets married, he/she needs to spend time with his/her own spouse and may have to stop doing things that the spouse does not enjoy. Unmarried sisters do not always realise, or cannot accept the fact, that when their siblings are married, they have responsibilities to their own families and may not be able to spend as much time with them as they would like to. Consequently, they may demand too much of their married siblings' time, money and energy.

This can also lead to 'in-law rivalry' in which the married sibling's spouse begins to resent the unmarried in-law's presence in their lives and unreasonable demands on them. One way to prevent this kind of rivalry is to regard the sibling's spouse not as an 'in-law' competing for attention, but as a brother or sister. There are some 'in-laws' who actually get on much better with each other than members of the original family, especially when there is a history of unresolved conflicts in the family of origin.

ESTABLISHING BOUNDARIES FOR THE FAMILY OF ORIGIN

Most relational problems involve a confusion of responsibility and ownership in our lives. They are problems of boundaries.

Meaning of Boundaries

"Just as homeowners set physical property lines around their land, we need to set mental, physical, emotional, and spiritual boundaries for our lives to help us distinguish what is our responsibility and what isn't."[1] It is generally accepted by psychologists and counsellors that the existence of clear boundaries is a necessary condition for healthy relationships.

Basic Boundary Conflicts Found in Families

The six boundary conflicts found between unmarried women and their families of origin listed below are taken from Cloud and Townsend, but the examples are my own.

Fusion – This happens when you are not able to stay separate from another person. For example, when your mother takes over the running of your life – from cooking to cleaning, to choice of life partner, career, finances and so on, your mother, not you, takes responsibility for your adult life.

Financial – You are not yet an adult financially either because (i) your parents provide everything that they desire for you but which you cannot afford – they pay for your flat and your car, and you are not sure if you want to give up these for a greater sense of independence, or (ii) you are perpetually in financial debt because of irresponsibility, drug or alcohol use, or out-of-control spending, and your parents continue to finance this road of failure and irresponsibility, thinking that "the next time, you'll do better."

The Perpetual Child Syndrome – You may be financially on your own, but allow your family of origin to perform certain life management functions. For example, you often hang out at your parents' house, vacation with them, drop off laundry, and eat many meals there. You are your parents' closest confidant, sharing everything with them. You are already in your thirties, but you still have not found your career niche, you have no savings, no retirement plan, and no health insurance.

Triangulation – This is the failure to resolve a conflict between two persons and the pulling in of a third to take sides. It goes something like this. Dorothy is angry with her brother Jim because he sold the family house without consulting her. She does not tell Jim herself. Instead she calls her sister Adeline and complains about Jim. Adeline is not only Dorothy's sister but also her best friend, and so she listens whenever Dorothy wants to play the 'triangle' game. By this time, Jim senses something is wrong as Dorothy has not called him for a few months, so he calls Adeline. Instead of trying to arrange a meeting for Dorothy and Jim to talk things through, Adeline now becomes the confidant of Jim as well. Adeline feels good that she is allowing both Dorothy and Jim to ventilate. In fact, she feels a bit self-righteous but she is not really helping them because they have not resolved their conflict.

Co-dependency with parents. While adult children should take care of their elderly parents (1 Timothy 5:3-4), they may have grown up taking responsibility for their parents who may be stuck in childish patterns of irresponsibility. The parents may not be really in need but are demanding or act like martyrs. When they are really in need, you may not have clear boundaries to determine what you can give and what you cannot give. This could lead to resentment.

Co-dependency with siblings. An adult sibling may behave irresponsibly and depend on another responsible adult sibling to avoid growing up and leaving the family. The tough issue here is the guilt and pressure that you feel because it is your brother or sister who is depending on you. Our families can tear down our best-built fences (needed for our emotional and spiritual health, not for selfish purposes) simply because they are 'family'.

Resolving Boundary Problems with Family Members

The steps in the resolution of boundary problems given below are adapted from Cloud and Townsend.[2]

Identify the Symptom. Look at your own life situation and see where boundary problems exist with your parents and siblings. Ask yourself: Where have you lost control of your boundaries? Then do something about it.

Identify the Conflict. For example, you may be taking responsibility *for* a sibling or parent instead of being responsible *to* them, and they do not appreciate it because they feel you are interfering too much in their lives.

Identify the Need that Drives the Conflict. Perhaps you are unable to be emotionally separate from your family of origin because you have a need to be loved, approved or accepted. Your family of origin may be so dysfunctional that they cannot meet these needs anyway and you may need to look to your brothers and sisters in God's family instead.

Take in and Receive the Good. Humble yourself, reach out to a good support system, and take in the good. Expect to get better. Learn to respond to and receive love, even if you are not comfortable with it at first.

Practise Boundary Skills. Learn to say yes, learn to say no, and learn to take control of your life. Practise these boundary skills in situations where you will be honoured and respected. Begin by saying "no" in your support group which loves and respects your boundaries.

Say "No" to the Bad. Avoid hurtful situations. When you are in the beginning stages of recovery, you need to avoid people who have abused and controlled you in the past. Be careful not to get sucked into a controlling situation again because your wish for reconciliation is so strong.

Forgive the Family Member who has Hurt You. When you refuse to forgive someone, you still want something from that person. Even if it is revenge that you want, it keeps you tied to him or her forever. If you forgive, you are freeing yourself, not the aggressor.

Respond, Don't React. The difference between responding and reacting is choice. When you are reacting, someone else is in control. When you respond, you are.

Learn to Live in Freedom and Responsibility, Not in Guilt. The best boundaries are loving ones. The person who has to remain forever in a protective mode is losing out on love and freedom. Boundaries in no way mean that you stop loving. They mean the opposite; you are gaining freedom to love. It is good to sacrifice and deny yourself for your family. But you need boundaries to make that choice.

CASE STUDIES

In this section, we will present four case studies of how some unmarried daughters honoured or failed to honour their parents and why.

Not Honouring Elderly Parents

Lian Choo is a 35-year-old woman who has everything a modern woman could ask for – money, status, career, power and love. Yet she is very unhappy and her life is punctured by anger, frustration and anxiety. She has long since abandoned her roots while seeking her pot of gold. She gives herself an English name – Jessica – in the hope that it would make her sound more 'modern' and make networking easier for her with her many foreign clients.

As an only child, Lian Choo had no choice but to let her elderly mother live with her. She certainly had the financial means to do so but she resented it.

Her mother was a devout Buddhist and she sacrificed food to her gods faithfully on a daily basis. As Lian Choo grew up, she considered this really old-fashioned and 'uncool'. She constantly mocked her mother for worshipping idols who could not possibly help her in any way. Nothing that the mother did was ever right – she made too much noise when she ate, she was too slow, she watched too much TV, she created a real mess every time she went to the toilet (even though the maid was quite happy to clean up after her).

The mother had learnt to accept things in her very slow stride. She tried to make herself invisible whenever she could. She hardly ever complained about anything even though the food she was served daily was Western food which she did not like. She just felt so grateful that her daughter gave her a room in her big house and the maid took good care of her. Lian Choo hardly had any time for her, but the mother rationalised that it was the price she had to pay for her daughter's success in life.

For Lian Choo, however, the mother stood in her way of her happiness. She was so old-fashioned and a constant unwelcome reminder of her past when she knew what it was to go hungry to bed, to be poor and to be looked down upon. So, like a decisive business woman, she made a unilateral decision to send her mother to a home for the elderly.

The mother was too grief-stricken to respond. Her one and only hope in life, her precious daughter, rejected her in her old age. What else was there to live for? When she arrived at the Christian home for the aged, she received a warm welcome. Slowly and very painfully, she gave up hope of ever seeing Lian Choo again. But God, in His goodness, showed mercy to her. In that very home for the aged, she indeed found happiness – from the family of God.

Honouring Your Parents but Putting Christ First in Your Life

When Jolyn first heard the gospel of Jesus Christ, she was only 18 years of age. She started to attend church with her Christian friends while she was still in school. Her parents were staunch Buddhists and had dedicated Jolyn to Guanyin, the Goddess of Mercy. They were very upset that Jolyn had forsaken her roots and gone after 'a foreign religion'. Jolyn wanted very much to be baptised but because of strong parental objections, she decided to wait till she turned 21. She was very close to her parents and continued to honour them in her daily life.

Her 21st birthday came and went. One day, unable to wait any longer, she approached her small group leader for advice. Her parents had softened a little in the previous three years but still objected to her baptism. She had to make a painful decision – to go ahead or postpone her baptism yet again. She felt that she had been honouring her parents in giving them time to accept her decision to get baptised, and she had waited for three years. Baptism would mean, for her as well as her parents, that there would be no turning back. Jolyn went ahead and was baptised.

Soon after her baptism, she became very ill with cancer. Although she wanted healing very much, and the whole church was praying for her healing, she did not recover and the Lord took His precious daughter home. On the day of Jolyn's funeral, to everyone's surprise, her parents announced that they wanted to get baptised. They decided to put their trust in Jesus because they had seen the peace in Jolyn's life even as she bravely fought the cancer. They knew it had to come from God. They also saw the love shown by her church members who were always there for her and who also comforted her parents every time they visited. That day, Jolyn's parents lost their only child; but God gave them many more brothers and sisters in the family of God. It all started when a teenager learned to honour God above her parents.

Honouring Parents in the Little Things of Life

Jane, an unmarried daughter became a Christian in her twenties. She lived with her parents who always seemed to be nagging her about washing her hair so late at night. They believed that this would cause her to get rheumatism in her old age. It is probably not true that washing one's hair late at night causes rheumatism but the Bible is silent on what is the best time to wash one's hair. Initially, Jane would argue heatedly against her parents, showing up their pre-scientific mindset. Her godmother saw her arguing one day and told her that she was not honouring them and not showing Christ-like character. Reluctantly, Jane agreed to change her personal habits so as not to aggravate her parents. That small step she took to inconvenience herself a little was enough to restore good relationships with her parents. She also learnt to listen more and not to argue so much with them, and that also strengthened the relationship between mother and daughter.

Honouring Parents in Their Advice about Career Choice

When Anne was finishing secondary school, she wanted very much to become a medical doctor but her parents objected because they thought there would be too many doctors in the family since her older brother was in medical school and her younger brothers intended to be doctors. Her mother also knew that although she had the intellectual capacity for medical studies, she lacked the physical stamina and emotional makeup to handle night calls, the sight of blood, deaths, and so on. In retrospect, Anne can see the wisdom of her mother's decision and she is glad that she did not go against her parents' wishes even though she could not really understand their reasons at that time. As she learned to honour her parents' decision, God honoured her so much more! He gave her one scholarship after another until she obtained a PhD in her twenties.

NOURISHING LOVE RELATIONSHIPS WITH FAMILY OF ORIGIN

The ultimate solution for all problems within the family of origin is love. This is easier said than done for love is a relationship that takes willingness, time and effort to nurture. Courting couples do not need excuses to spend time with each other. They just want to, and so find the time to be with each other. With the family of origin, however, some unmarried women may be so traumatised and feel so unloved that they neither have the desire nor emotional energy to try to change anything. It is only the grace of God, the way in which He loves each one of us and freely forgives us unconditionally that can bring a ray of hope to families in distress.

In nourishing love relationships with our family of origin, we need to do the following:

1. Ask what we can give, not what we can get out of the relationship.
2. Honour our parents.
3. Enjoy our natural bonding with our siblings but give each other space. Respect each other's boundaries and do not violate them, even if we are the older sibling.
4. Do not allow the sibling rivalry of the past to cast a shadow on our present relationships.
5. Help to take care of our nieces and nephews, but do not try to run their lives or that of their parents.
6. Celebrate birthdays and anniversaries together.

CONCLUSION

Among the network of relationships that God has designed for the single woman, the family of origin is perhaps the most important. It is the one network that helps to explain who we are today, why we relate in certain ways, and why we may be caught in an endless cycle of relational failure. It is also the only network of relationships for which we have no choice. We are born into families. We do not get to choose our brothers and sisters. In some ways, it is the same with God's family – the church, except that we enter into this family through our personal choice. The network of relationships that is easiest to dismantle is that with our colleagues. If we dislike our colleagues, we can look for another job and never have to see them again. But even then, if we have unresolved relational problems, we will carry them into our next job, even though our old colleagues are no longer around to 'bug' us.

If we come from dysfunctional families, we do not need to lose hope as God is in the business of changing lives and He has a very impressive track record. Stormie Omartian's books, for example, contain many stories of dysfunctional families which only God could have changed and He did.

If we grew up in a Christian family which practised biblical values, we are indeed very blessed and may have been spared a lot of pain and despair. But even so, there is no place for complacency. Many unmarried women who have grown up in Christian homes still suffer from relational failures because they have not abandoned sinful patterns of behaviour which they may have inherited and learned from their parents and ancestors.

God is the best relational guru that I know. He is the only one who can fix our relational problems with our families. But we need to co-operate with Him and give Him permission to work with the broken pieces of our fragmented lives.

9

Connection with CHURCH FAMILY

Apart from her family of origin, the Asian woman who is a Christian is connected to her church family. If her family of origin is small, and many Asian families are now quite small, with only one uncle or aunt, and only one sibling, she may not be able to experience what it is like to have a brother or sister In a healthy and growing church, however, she can learn how to relate to men and women as brothers and sisters.

THE BIBLICAL TEACHING ABOUT THE CHURCH

The Bible uses many images to describe the Church: the temple of God, the Israel of God, the building of God, the body of Christ, the 'oikos' or household of God, and the bride of Christ. Of these, the three that pertain to family are the body of Christ, the household of God and the bride of Christ. We shall deal with the first two in this chapter and the last in Chapter 14 on 'Preparing for the Ultimate Wedding'.

The Body of Christ

The 'body of Christ' is used in the Bible with a wide range of connotations.

Christ is the Head of the Body.

In Colossians 1:18, Paul states in no uncertain terms: "He (Christ) is the head of the body, the church; He is the beginning and the firstborn from among the dead, so that in everything He might have the supremacy." This headship points to an organic and living relationship that Christ has with his people. He is the source of life and power to them so that they are totally dependent on Him for their very existence. He is also the one who exercises loving control and headship over them. The risen Christ is the head; "he is the beginning and *the firstborn from among the dead*."

Christ is *the* head, and not *a* head, of the body. His headship is the foundation of all relationships within the church. A chicken is killed when its head is chopped off. Its body parts may remain intact but without the head, its life soon ebbs away. In the same way, the Church must depend on Christ as its source of life and its supremacy, or it will be like a headless chicken. It can still run around for a little while but it has no more life.

Unity in Diversity

"The body is a unit, though it is made up of many parts; and though all its parts are many, they form one body. So it is with Christ. For we were all baptised by *one* Spirit into *one* body – whether Jews or Greeks, slave or free – and we were all given the *one* Spirit to drink" (1 Corinthians 12:12-13).

Note that the biblical emphasis is on 'unity in diversity' and not 'diversity in unity'. Oneness in Christ cannot be sacrificed to accommodate the dizzy diversity of opinions on matters of faith and conduct found in some churches today. The body of Christ can only function as a unit when all are baptised by one Spirit – the Holy Spirit. It is not a unity that has to be generated from man-made initiatives. The unity is already given. Nor should unity be confused with uniformity. Where true unity exists through the Holy Spirit, people are free to exercise different gifts in the body, according to what God has given them.

Mutuality

Apart from being one body in Christ, we belong to one another for "in Christ we who are many form one body, and each member *belongs* to all the others" (Romans 12:5). This belonging does not depend on whether a woman is married or not. As each member belongs to all the others, it also means that there is no place for individualism. Mutuality is a keynote to healthy relationships in the church. We exist for one another and no longer for ourselves.

Freedom to Exercise Gifts

Within the body which is one, there is a true diversity of gifts. As the church is much bigger than our family of origin, we can expect a greater diversity of gifts than is found within a single family. This diversity must be viewed as an asset rather than a liability. It is tempting to do things our own way, to judge others according to our own standards, and to associate only with those who are like us, in upbringing, personality, temperament and so on. But to do so would be to limit ourselves severely, to our own disadvantage. Every member of our church is a gift to us, and we often learn the most from those who are most different from us, provided we can accept differences as God's gift to His body.

Growth

The body of Christ is also characterised by growth. Writing about the false teachers in Colossae, Paul warns that "he (the false teacher) has lost connection with the Head, from whom the whole body, *supported and held together* by its ligaments and sinews, grows as God causes it to grow" (Colossians 2:19). Note two important points about growth here. First, the whole body *grows as God causes it to grow*. We cannot bring about growth through new initiatives or growth programmes. Second, the whole body is supported and held together by its ligaments and sinews – we grow together, not on our own. If one part grew at the expense of another, the body would no longer be a body but a monster.

The 'Oikos' or Household

Reinstating the Asian Concept of Family in Church

In English usage today, we differentiate between the 'nuclear family' and the 'extended family'. Western-educated Asians tend to think of their family primarily as 'spouse + children', and every other family relationship as secondary or extended. It is this distinction that leaves the singles feeling that they have no place in their families, and by analogy, no place in church, since that is defined as the family of God.

In traditional Asian culture, however, family is primarily family of origin and married couples would talk of their parents, aunts and uncles, siblings, cousins, etc. not as 'extended family' but just as 'family'.

This traditional Asian concept of family is much closer to the biblical concept of the church as the 'oikos' or household, which included several generations AND slaves living with them! A call to return to the biblical concept of household would mean a call to return to thinking of family in the broadest sense. In church, we are ALL brothers and sisters, whether we are married or not. This inclusiveness would help singles feel more welcome, rather than thinking narrowly of families to mean just 'father, mother and children', and narrowly restricting ministry opportunities to such families.

Small Groups Based on 'Oikos' Concept

The secret to successful growth in a church lies in its small groups which are based on the 'oikos' concept. In para-church organisations, small groups are homogenous. For example, a Nurses' Christian Fellowship includes only nurses – they are all in the same profession, have had the same training, and may be quite close in age. Such homogenous groups have their advantages but in the Bible, small groups are based on the 'oikos' or household concept. According to this concept, a small group is like a family. Learning to relate well to different members of the family requires crossing from one generation to another – for the grandparents to understand the grandchildren and vice versa – and to accept differences in taste, not only of food and such survival issues, but also in the way we worship. Some churches , realising the importance of the 'oikos' concept, even make it possible for three generations to worship together by offering inter-generational services in which there is something relevant and meaningful for each generation.

Inter-generational Services

Inter-generational services encourage families to worship together. This is important because single mothers who feel that their children need a father's touch can worship together with the children's god-parents. Single women who may feel that they do not belong can integrate much better as unmarried aunts or unmarried sisters in quite a natural way as families worship together. This is truly a biblical way of 'setting the lonely in families'. Some families may have one spouse who is a Christian but the other one is not. Some spouses started by following their partner to church for the sake of the children or grandchildren and eventually putting their faith in Christ.

Domestic Helpers as Part of the Household

In the more affluent countries of Asia, it is very common for domestic helpers to live with the family they are working for. Such helpers are an essential part of the household or 'oikos' and while we need to apply the biblical guidelines about how slaves and masters should relate to one another, they are also to be treated as part of the family. This is already put into practice even in non-Christian homes. Children are taught to address such helpers not by name but as 'aunty', which is an indication that they are considered part of the family. It is true that the word 'aunty' could also be just a term used by younger people in addressing older people but behind the use of 'aunty' and 'uncle', there is definitely the implication that they are family.

LIVING OUT THE CHURCH AS FAMILY

In the letter to the Ephesians, Paul makes it clear that believers, both individually and corporately, both single and married, have responsibilities first to Christ as Lord and then to one another. They "must no longer live as the Gentiles do, in the futility of their thinking" (Ephesians 4:17). For the Christian postmodern woman living in Asia today, this means that she must not live any more like unbelievers. Her mind is to be renewed by

Christ and the values that He has taught in Scripture. She is not to live in the futility of the thought patterns and lifestyles promoted by the world.

The key to all relationships is mutual submission. As Paul puts it in Ephesians 5:21, "submit to one another out of reverence for Christ." This verse actually serves as the introduction to the relationships that follow: wives and husbands (5:22-33), children and parents (6:1-4), slaves and masters (or the employee and the employer in today's world) (6:5-9). Many miss this very important point that mutual submission out of reverence for Christ is the key to healthy relationships because in most translations of the Bible in English, verse 21 comes at the end of the previous section rather than the beginning of the next section on relationships.

Of all the relationships listed in Ephesians 5:22-6:9, only one – the relationship between husband and wife – does not apply to the single woman. All the other relationships apply both to the married and the single woman.

Wives are to submit to their husbands as to the Lord (5:22); husbands are to love their wives just as Christ loved the church and gave himself up for her (5:25); children are to obey their parents in the Lord (6:1); fathers are not to exasperate their children but instead bring them up in the training and instruction of the Lord (6:4); slaves are to obey their earthly masters just as they would obey Christ (6:5); masters are to treat their slaves in the same way as Christ is both the slaves' master and theirs.

RELATIONSHIPS WITHIN THE CHURCH (TITUS 2)

In the Pastoral Epistles (especially 1 and 2 Timothy, and Titus) written by the Apostle Paul, there are clear guidelines about how specific groups of people should conduct themselves.

Older Men

In order to build good and healthy relationships with older men in the church, single women should think of them not as potential life partners if they are unmarried, but as fathers and older brothers. This should surely take some of the pressure off the single woman who may be too self-conscious for her own good if she regards every older unmarried man as a potential life partner. The unmarried older man also knows that he could be hunted down ruthlessly by female singles, like an endangered species! He cannot be his best if he is worried all the time about being sought after by every single woman looking for a husband.

If single women would accept their God-given role as daughters and younger sisters to older men, they can indeed be used by God to help older men become what God has intended for them: to be temperate, worthy of respect, self-controlled, and sound in faith, in love and in endurance (Titus 2:2).

Older Women

If single women treat older women as mothers and older sisters, they can help the older women to become what God has intended for them. If they themselves are the older women, they should accept their age graciously, and not panic about the strong likelihood of remaining single as the years slip by, but instead ask God to help them become what they are expected to be and do: "to be reverent in the way they live, not to be slanderous or addicted to much wine, but to teach what is good. Then, they can train the younger women to… be self-controlled and pure… to be kind… so that no one will malign the word of God" (Titus 2:3-5).

In all these instructions, there is no discrimination between married women and single women. Older women have a God-given role to fulfil in the church, whether they are married or single.

Younger Men

It is now quite common to find women marrying younger men, even though Asian society still finds this hard to accept. However desperate a single woman may be to get married, she should treat younger unmarried men firstly as younger brothers or sons, and only seriously consider them as potential life partners if God gives them the green light.

Older women, whether married or single, have a role to play in helping younger men become what God intends them to be. They are to encourage the younger men "to be self-controlled. In everything set them an example by doing what is good. In your teaching, show integrity, seriousness and soundness of speech that cannot be condemned" (Titus 2:6-8). Again, the Scriptures make it clear that older women have a God-given role to fulfil in their relationships with younger men, and this role does not depend on whether they are married or not, but simply on the fact that they are older women.

Younger Women

While it is only the married women who can teach younger women to love their husbands and children, and to be subject to their husbands, every older woman, married or single, can be a role model to younger women on how to be self-controlled and pure, to be busy at home, and to be kind.

Children

From the biblical perspective, the single woman should not have any biological children since sex outside marriage is strictly forbidden. However, she has a role to play as a 'spiritual' mother to her godchildren and to be role models of contented singles to them – something that her godchildren's parents cannot possibly demonstrate.

INDISPENSABLE RELATIONSHIPS

Leonard Sweet has given a very comprehensive description of certain indispensable relationships.[1] He lists 11 such relationships. For each, he gives an example of a character in the Bible, describes what the relationship is about, and why it is indispensable. The fact that most of these characters are men rather than women makes no difference to the relationship concerned.

1. Your Editor

   This is someone who edits your life to improve upon it. The role of this editor is basically the same as what I have described as accountability partner in Chapter 7. A biblical example is the prophet Nathan who pointed his finger at David for his adultery with Bathsheba (2 Samuel 11 and 12) and was thus instrumental in David's repentance as described in Psalm 51.

2. Your True Friend
   A biblical example is Jonathan, the son of King Saul, who became a true friend to David and saved his life on several occasions.

3. Your Motivator[2]
   This is someone who motivates you forward to go to what God is calling you to do so that you can receive peace in your life. A biblical example is Jethro, father-in-law to Moses, who moved Moses forward quite a few times with his practical wisdom.

4. Your Protégé
   A biblical example is Timothy who became Paul's protégé.

5. Your Encourager
   A biblical example is Barnabas who encouraged many, including the Apostles and especially Paul.

6. Your Mentor
   Two biblical examples are Peter (to John Mark) and Paul (to Silas and Timothy).

7. Your Back Coverer
   This is someone who protects you from back-biting and back-stabbing. A biblical example is Deborah the judge (Judges 4 and 5).

8. Your Reject
   A biblical example is Zaccheus who had to climb a tree to see Jesus as he was hated and rejected by all. Jesus was completely at home with people like that for He came to call 'sinners' to repentance. Single

women need to make friends with people like that to be in touch with the reality of sin.

9. Your Little One
   A biblical example is Rhoda, the little servant girl who worked in the home of Mary in Jerusalem. When Peter was imprisoned, the Christians met in Mary's home to pray for his release. Their prayer was answered and Peter came straight to the house after his release. But it was Rhoda who recognised his voice and believed it was him. Single women need to relate to children like Rhoda who can become their role models of simple, trusting faith that God answers prayer.

10. Your Rich and Poor Friends
    A biblical example of a rich woman who used her wealth to further God's kingdom is Lydia (Acts 16:11-15 and subsequent passages in Acts) and a biblical example of an abjectly poor beggar is Lazarus (Luke 16:19-31). Both Lydia and Lazarus should be our VIPs so that we can know and understand both the world of the rich and the poor, and how to relate to them better.

11. The Holy Spirit
    All of these relationships are important for the single woman. As the years slip by, she may be inclined to relate only to her own safe network of friends. These may be mostly single women like her. Some of these, for example your 'Zaccheus', you would never find unless you look for them consciously. Jesus was single but He looked out for such people and associated with them so closely that the religious leaders of the day quickly nicknamed him 'the friend of sinners'. In Jesus we have a good role model of all that we can be in our relationships.

For those single women who may be feeling sorry for themselves because they have been deprived of that ONE relationship (husband-wife) that they so much long for, may this list be a reminder that these indispensable relationships cannot all be found in just one's spouse. On the contrary, a single woman may have more time and opportunities to develop some of these indispensable relationships. And her life should be fuller and richer because of these relationships!

RECOMMENDATIONS BY KRISTIN AUNE

What the Church Can Do for the Single Woman

Kristin Aune conducted research (based on interviews, questionnaires and letter testimonies) on never-married evangelical women in Britain for an M.A. dissertation in 1998.[3] Although her research reflects a typically Western perspective on women, emphasising rights more than responsibilities, her recommendations to the church on how it can understand and appreciate the single women better are still applicable today, not only just in the West but in Asia as well. I will, therefore list her recommendations below:

1. Treat single women as individuals rather than as a homogenous group.
2. Give them a voice within the church and listen to what they say.
3. Let them use their wide range of gifts to serve God and the church.
4. Address and debate the subject of women's roles in church and seek to involve single women in leadership.
5. Employ single women as pastoral workers and develop female support and mentoring systems.
6. Seek to be a community in which all, single and married, female and male, are involved, loved, supported and needed. Encourage the development of close friendships.
7. Think through biblical ways in which single women's sexuality can be expressed and celebrated.
8. Do not put marriage on a pedestal. Be honest about its advantages and disadvantages.
9. Develop an evangelistic focus on singles in their various states.
10. Teach both single people and the whole church about the benefits of singleness.

MY RECOMMENDATIONS

The focus of Aune's study is on the rights of single women – they have a right to be treated as individuals, to be heard, to serve God and the church with their wide range of gifts, to leadership in the church, to work as pastoral workers, and to express their sexuality.

While this focus may be important for churches which have no place for single women, an over-emphasis on rights, at the expense of responsibilities, can be unhealthy not just for the church but even more so for the single woman. Her freedom and independence are valuable gifts that come with singleness but these gifts can be abused. The single woman can become so self-centred that she expects the church to meet her every need but feels less convicted about using her gifts and time to meet the needs of others. Ultimately, I believe that the key to living happily as a single lies in having healthy relationships, as emphasised in this book. Giving them their rights indiscriminately may actually be more harmful to them in the long run.

What the Single Woman Can Do for the Church

The focus of my discussion on the church family is more on what the singles can receive from and contribute to their brothers and sisters in the church family rather than on how they deserve to be treated. This has already been discussed in the preceding pages. God's church will be glorified when non-believers see how the believers love one another and not vie for positions within the church, especially those that appear to carry more clout like pastoral workers, missionaries, and evangelists.

HOW THE CHURCH CAN SUPPORT SINGLES IN THEIR JOURNEY

Having served in church as a single woman in almost every ministry from teaching Sunday school to leading worship and preaching, I realise that there is a big gap between how the church sees the singles and how the singles see the church. I believe that this gap must be closed for the mutual benefit of both the church and the singles. It may take years to close the gap in churches which are totally family-oriented and quite clueless about the struggles and needs of singles. But we have to make a start. I humbly suggest a three-pronged approach as outlined below.

Build a Community in Which All can Grow Together

In this kind of community, single and married, male and female, young and old are all involved, loved, supported and needed.

Encourage the Development of Close Relationships

Many singles have learnt to develop the closest relationship of intimacy with God. In quite a few churches, they are the ones who most effectively lead others to a closer walk with God by the way they model 'closeness' to Christ, much like the way that Mary in the Bible just sat at Jesus' feet, listening to what He had to say.

Do Not Put Marriage on a Pedestal

Be honest about its advantages and disadvantages. This message is best lived out rather than taught from the pulpit. Transparency and vulnerability should not only be expected from singles, but also from married people. Just because a person is married does not mean that he or she has solved all problems. In a good marriage, joys are doubled and sorrows halved. But there are many marriages, even Christian ones, in which joys are halved because of the inability to genuinely love each other and in which sorrows are doubled because the couple has not learnt the view from the Cross.

The myth that it is better to be unhappily married than to be happily single can only be debunked if the church sends out a clear message that God calls some to be married but others to be single (whether they appreciate the calling or not is beside the point). One is not better than another. This way, singles will not be encouraged to think of themselves either as 'super-singles' or as 'half-sized Christians', both of which are distortions of the truth about singles.

Teach Both Single People and the Whole Church about the Calling to Singleness

Many churches already run groups for singles and teach them that God may call them to singleness. For those singles who already know this and have embraced the gift with joy, it is like preaching to the converted when the teaching is confined to groups of single people.

The whole church needs to hear both from married people, as well as singles, from men as well as women, of the calling to singleness and how to be obedient to this calling as part of the calling to follow Christ who is the supreme example of a life lived in singleness but always in communion with God.

If singles are the only ones preaching the message of singleness as a calling and a gift, it can be perceived by the married ones as either totally irrelevant to them or worse, as a matter of 'self consolation'.

If married people are the only ones preaching this message, it may be a case of 'the grass looking greener on the other side of the fence' as they would have very little experience of what it actually feels like to be single year after year.

The best thing that the church can do for single women is to help them dispel myths about marriage so that they are better prepared for marriage if it comes their way, as well as for continued singleness.

10

CONNECTION WITH COLLEAGUES AT WORK

This chapter deals with a very important connection for the single woman. It is her connection with her colleagues at work. This is perhaps the most important connection for the single woman as she spends most of her waking hours at her work place. She may even spend all her time at work – leaving home early in the morning and returning only late at night just to sleep. She may use work as an excuse for not thinking through the critical issues about singleness, or she may work such long hours, not because the job is demanding, but as an escape from loneliness.

THE BIBLICAL PERSPECTIVE OF WORK

The Bible has a high view of work. Genesis, the first book of the Bible, begins with an account of God at work. He created the universe, and the first man and woman, and made plans for Adam and Eve to work in the Garden of Eden. In one of the Psalms celebrating the Creation, the Psalmist describes the heavens as "the work of Your (God's) fingers" (Psalm 8:3).

Work Before the Fall[1]

Work has always been part of God's plan for humanity. He planned for people to "be fruitful and increase in number; fill the earth and subdue it. Rule over the fish of the sea and the birds of the air and over every living creature that moves on the ground" (Genesis 1:28). He wanted human beings to bring the earth under their control and to manage it responsibly.

Work After the Fall

Difficulties with Work

One of the effects of the Fall was that work became difficult and painful. "Cursed is the ground because of you; through painful toil you will eat of it all the days of your life. It will produce thorns and thistles for you, and you will eat the plants of the field. By the sweat of your brow you will eat your food until you return to the ground, since from it you were taken; for dust you are and to dust you will return" (Genesis 3:17-19). Work itself was not a curse on man, but the difficulties with work are the result of the Fall.

Disowning Responsibilities

The boundary problem of not taking responsibility for what is ours started in the Garden of Eden when Adam and Eve tried to pass the blame to another for their own sinfulness. Adam blamed Eve; Eve blamed the serpent (Genesis 3:11-13). They were disowning their responsibility and blaming another. This tendency to blame one another is a key problem at work.

The Purpose of Work

What is the purpose of paid employment for the single woman? Economic necessity – to have money for food, clothing and the basic necessities of life – is the primary reason for work.

Paul, in his letter to the Thessalonians warns them against idleness, which is defined as 'not working'. He gave them this rule which we should also observe. "If a man will not work, he shall not eat" (2 Thessalonians 3:10).

The Routine of Work

The routine of work is ordained by the Creator Himself. In describing the orderliness of God's creation, the Psalmist includes going out to work. "Then man goes out to his work, to his labour until evening" (Psalm

104:23). Once we get used to the routine of work, it may seem boring, but boredom is not so much a consequence of the nature of the work but of the attitude of the worker.

Attitude Towards Work

The first attitude that will see us through the unpleasant politics that goes on in the marketplace is to focus on God and not on status, recognition, monetary returns or other materialistic rewards. In 1 Thessalonians 2:4-6, Paul admonished women and men to seek in all pursuits to please God. God should not just be confined to church on Sundays. Ask Him to go with us and help us in the marketplace from Mondays to Fridays.

If we focus on pleasing God, He will enable us not only to please others and meet their needs but also to bring honour to Him through our work. In other words, God is the source of wisdom and strength for us to do our work in a way that will honour Christ. The Lord will go with us to our jobs, and He is totally capable of helping us with any problems. He can make an enormous difference in our focus, attitude and motivations (Colossians 3:23, 24).

At the marketplace, we should seek to be the best that we can be. We should work with all our hearts, not with an eye on the clock. This, however, does not mean that work becomes our religion nor that work takes over all of our lives. The single woman has to resist the temptation of working 24/7 simply because she has nothing else to do. For her, as much as for the married woman, taking regular periods of rest and using up her quota of annual leave are vital to her physical, emotional and spiritual health.

In work situations where excellence is rewarded and mistakes severely punished , there is a great temptation to strive for perfection. Excellence is a laudable aim at work but striving for perfection in an imperfect world, with imperfect people, brings about unnecessary stress not only for the perfectionist but also those she works with. By focusing on God's unconditional love, we can be set free from demanding perfection of ourselves. Jesus Himself finished His life work without healing every person who was sick or preaching to everyone who was lost (John 4:34). Our first challenge as single career women is to fear the Lord, and then order our work according to His priorities and plans.

A CAREER WOMAN WHO HONOURED CHRIST

Lydia, who is first introduced in Acts Chapter 16, is a good role model for women who work in the marketplace. She was probably married, but that is irrelevant as no mention is made of a husband or children. There is nothing she did which the single woman cannot do. She was a wealthy and influential businesswoman who sold articles dyed purple, a prized colour made from certain molluscs. She probably had a spacious home that could accommodate many guests and she probably had servants to meet their needs. This must have been a rare achievement in her day. She surely must have been an intelligent, hard-working woman with great entrepreneurial skills and the gift of hospitality.

Once she became a believer, what had been hers before – home, business, and possessions – now belonged to the Lord. She had a new partner, the Lord Jesus, a new purpose to serve Him, and a new satisfaction in seeking to be more effective and successful in order to glorify the Lord.

As soon as she believed, she invited Paul and Silas to use her home as the meeting place for true worshippers. They no longer had to meet at the riverside because Lydia opened her home to the church. And it was through her home that the gospel spread to the continent of Europe. God used this dedicated businesswoman and her resources for His purposes in a big way.

BIBLICAL TEACHING ON WORK RELATIONSHIPS

Motivation for Work

The Bible teaches that in everything, Christians ought to serve others as if they were serving God himself. Our motivation for work should not be for personal gain such as to get that much sought-after promotion. These are worldly motives which are unworthy of a Christian. Our ultimate goal in life is to please God, not men, and to look for God's reward, rather than immediate, earthly rewards. If the market place is full of Christians who are God-pleasers rather than flatterers and men-pleasers, the atmosphere of the work place will be so much better.

Relationships with Our Superiors

The people in positions of authority are part of God's plan for orderliness in the world. The Bible teaches that we are to submit ourselves to the people who have risen to those positions of directing work to be done. To rebel against that authority is to rebel against God's order, which will bring God's judgment on us. The single woman working in the marketplace needs to live by this principle, however difficult it may be to implement and however counter-cultural it may seem to be, in a generation that rejects and challenges authority.

The authority over us may be incompetent or inadequate in some way, but that authority is still to be respected. Obviously there are people in positions of authority who should never be there. That was also the case when Paul wrote his letter to the Romans. Yet he taught them that "everyone must submit himself to the governing authorities, for there is no authority except that which God has established..." (Romans 13:1).

We may find it extremely difficult to respect the *people* in authority perhaps because they are not worthy of respect. But we must respect their *authority*. Only when that authority would lead us to compromise Christian principles should we refuse to submit. As Jesus himself taught us in Matthew 22:21, we are to "give to Caesar what is Caesar's, and to God what is God's."

Scripture gives clear direction for relating to those in authority over us, including our employer. In 1 Peter 2:18, Peter instructs slaves to submit themselves to their masters with all respect, not only to those who are good and considerate, but also to those who are harsh. This same principle applies to the employee-employer relationship today.

Submission is yielding to the authority of another. Respecting someone means, in part, to treat him or her with consideration. Both can be done contrary to feelings, by an act of the will, especially when empowered by the Holy Spirit. The employee should perform job-related tasks with excellence, even when they have been treated unfairly. Peter goes on to say that it is commendable to bear up under unfair treatment, for that kind of suffering finds favour with God (1 Peter 2:20).

Submission to authority changes the employee for the better. When she applies this principle to difficult management relationships, God changes her thinking and her attitude so that much of the stress and frustration of the relationship are relieved. God has told us that His yoke is easy and His burden is light (Matthew 11:28). Accepting it from God's hands and letting Him guide our reactions – even to the point of suffering from unfair treatment – are easier than the 'normal' human reactions of anger, bitterness and vengeance, which are discussed in Chapters 3, 4 and 5.

Relationships with Our Peers

The basic principles governing healthy relationships with family members and church members also apply to peers in the workplace. Here are two important principles which are particularly relevant to the workplace. First, think of what you can give rather than 'what's in it for me' as the Bible teaches that "it is more blessed to give than to receive" (Acts 20:35). Second, help others when they become burdened by work problems (Galatians 6:1-5).

Relationships with our peers can be ruined by pride or envy. If we do well at work and our peers are struggling, it is tempting to look down on them and their abilities. On the other hand, if we are struggling and our peers seem to do so well, we must guard against envy. In the workplace, envy can rear its ugly head in many ways. We may envy our colleagues' success, promotion, salary increases, position within the company and so on.

Relationships with Our Subordinates

Women who rise to positions of authority, especially if they rise very quickly or suddenly, often become the target of envy from their work colleagues. Sometimes, there is nothing they can do about this except to go the second mile to strengthen relationships with their subordinates. But very often, relationships with subordinates turn sour because the woman boss is not as kind as the male boss. Her attention to detail can make her come over as being unnecessarily picky.

In order to develop good relationships with their subordinates, single women who have risen to the top of the corporate ladder need to guard especially against the following attitudes which can destroy good relationships.

First, guard against an intimidating or threatening attitude towards subordinates. This is very common with women bosses who feel insecure, and single women who have not learnt to be accountable to anyone can be particularly insecure in their new-found position.

Second, an authoritarian attitude especially towards male subordinates can really destroy previously good relationships. Unfortunately, the same single women who resent authoritarian attitudes in their fathers and older brothers tend to become authoritarian themselves when they become bosses.

Third, the single woman who becomes the boss must guard against unreal expectations from her subordinates at the workplace. The married woman who has been up all night nursing a sick child or worried about her husband's frequent travel overseas is unlikely to be as dedicated to her work as the single woman for whom work is everything. Of course, there are also married women who make work their main aim in life and there are single women who are too distracted to work efficiently because they are on a man-hunt all the time or living an overly full social life.

SOLVING COMMON PROBLEMS IN THE MARKETPLACE

Cloud and Townsend, in their classic work entitled *Boundaries*, have a list of the common problems in the marketplace and give case studies of how these problems were solved when people took responsibility for their own work and set clear limits. Their case studies are helpful but some boundaries are difficult or impossible to implement in Asian society, while other factors like 'saving face' and 'guanxi' (the Chinese word for 'connections') are important considerations in Asia. I will, therefore, use Asian case studies to illustrate the nature of each problem, and suggest some Asian methods of solving these problems.

Bearing Another Person's Responsibility

Jennifer works as an insurance agent. Most of her team members work hard and manage to meet their targets except for Sylvia, who happens to be her younger cousin and the daughter of the CEO.

Without realising it, Jennifer would often do Sylvia's job for her, even to the extent of meeting her clients for her. She was also afraid of upsetting Sylvia in case she reported her unhelpfulness to her father who had the power to dismiss her without good reason.

Sylvia took advantage of Jennifer and depended on her to meet her own targets while doing very little herself. This went on for several months until Jennifer's own performance started to be adversely affected.

Fortunately, her team leader, John, noticed this and invited her in to his office for a chat. At first, Jennifer was reluctant to share her problems as she felt she would be betraying a family member. But she finally told him the truth.

John did not try to get Jennifer and Sylvia together to talk things through. That would cause Jennifer to 'lose face'. He also wisely avoided conflict within the family, which might also affect his own career prospects. Instead, he tactfully put in place a one-day seminar for all his team members and taught them about boundaries at work and how such boundaries help to increase productivity.

Jennifer took ownership of her problem. She realised that she was not helping anyone by doing Sylvia's work. She had a heart-to-heart talk with her younger cousin. She told her that for the sake of the family's reputation, they would both need to improve their performance. This meant that she could no longer do her cousin's work for her.

At first, Sylvia was very angry and threatened to tell her father. But later, Sylvia began to realise that her older cousin was also taking responsibility for her own poor performance and not blaming her.

They decided to try out some new work routines for a month. Sylvia would do her own work, deal with her own clients, and also do all the necessary paper work. It was very difficult for Sylvia at first but Jennifer spent one evening a week with her to guide her with the paper work and to review her dealings with her clients. Within a month, there were smiles all round as both Sylvia and Jennifer's performance improved. They each took responsibility for their own work; no one was saddled with another person's responsibility.

Misplaced Priorities

Some problems at work arise from misplaced priorities. Selena worked as a secretary in the sales department of a multi-national corporation. Her work station looked exemplary at any hour of the day – neat, well-organised, and professional. She got on very well with everyone and so far, no one had complained about her. So it came as a big shock to her when, at the end of her one-month probation, the boss gave her a strong warning that unless she did better, she would be dismissed.

What were Selena's problems? First, she had not learnt to say "no". She did whatever she was asked to do – whether the request came from her boss or colleague. She even did errands for the office boy. Soon, she could not cope with the sheer volume of work. Most of it was so rushed that it was poorly done.

Second, Selena had not learnt to prioritise the work requests according to her own criteria. Instead, she allowed the pushy bosses to get priority. Whoever shouted the loudest got her attention the most. There was one boss who always marked everything IMMEDIATE and his work always got done first but he was still not happy because he also expected perfect work which, of course, Selena could not produce as she was still learning the ropes.

Selena's third problem was that she had no idea about how to plan her time wisely and get rid of time wasters. She was always typing, sending emails and filing non-stop, yet her work was always unfinished.

The warning from the boss shook Selena as she wanted her job badly. She got some advice from an older colleague who taught her three basic principles about how to prioritise her work effectively. She put these into practice very conscientiously and within a few months, she was so efficient that she received her first promotion.

First, Selena learnt to say "no" to anything that she was not obliged to do. For example, she started to say "no" to the office boy's requests to buy lunch for other staff while she was out at lunch. It was not part of her contract. She studied her job description carefully and focused on only what she was required to do.

Second, Selena learnt to tell the difference between the urgent and the important. Certain jobs marked urgent or immediate were not really as urgent as others which were actually more important but not marked as such. She even put the following sign on her desk, "Poor planning on your part does not constitute an emergency on my part." She worked out her priorities according to her own criteria: A, B and C. Priority A requests would get done within the day; B within the week, and C within the month. If there were too many Priority A requests in one day, she would go and see her boss and ask which could be moved to B.

Third, Selena did an hourly time log of what she did every day for about a month and soon discovered that she needed to improve her time management. Certain time-consuming but routine jobs like photocopying could be passed on to the office boy as that was part of his job. She learnt to group her activities in such a way so as to save time. For example, she would block off time to write emails instead of handling them one by one as they came in. She would also do filing only after she had a stack of documents instead of doing it one by one. Grouping activities together saved her a lot of time. She also got rid of time-wasters like being distracted by pop-up advertisements while doing email.

Working Too Much Overtime

Irene had just returned from studying overseas. She landed her first job at a very prestigious school. However, she soon discovered, to her horror, that she could not possibly complete what she was expected to do and found herself working longer and longer hours each day. Of course there was no extra pay for overtime work. Irene never complained about this because she enjoyed her work.

However, Irene soon discovered that she had no life apart from working long hours at the school. She no longer had time for all the things she enjoyed – rock climbing, scuba diving and other outdoor activities. Her boyfriend threatened to leave her if she did not manage to find the time to see him. Even her health was beginning to be affected. She constantly had migraine attacks and sleepless nights, and her blood pressure was dangerously high.

With the help of her boyfriend, she took the following bold steps to build boundaries at work.

She decided how much overtime she was willing to do. Of course, during the examination period and the weeks preceding that, she was prepared to work longer hours to help the students. But she made it the exception, not the rule.

She wrote out a job description of what she had to do every month.

She made a list of all the tasks she had to complete by the end of each month and ranked them in order of importance.

She discussed her workload with the principal and pointed out gently, but firmly, that she could not handle it without doing so much overtime, which she was not prepared to do.

Irene had thought through the priorities of her life and determined that work was not going to swallow up everything else. She was prepared to find another job if necessary. She had earlier put some money in an 'emergency fund' to tide her through periods of unemployment. The principal appreciated her boldness to speak up. No other teacher had dared to negotiate working hours. They just put up with it but grumbled incessantly, behind the principal's back of course. Their work made a turn for the worse. They lost interest in teaching and in the students and just went to school every day to get their pay packet at the end of the month.

When we are clear about how much time we can reasonably spend at work without affecting our physical, emotional, mental and spiritual health, our work will be more efficient. Others may also be helped in the process.

Difficult Colleagues

There will always be difficult colleagues at any work place. They may be driven and drive others crazy with their driven. Cloud and Townsend mention a very important principle called The Law of Power: "You only have the power to change yourself. You can't change another person."

The solution to difficult colleagues is not to try and change them but to deny them the power to control our lives emotionally.

Pearl was the youngest and least experienced employee in her company. But she had practised boundaries in her home and in her church, and she know how to put these 'boundary laws' in place when she started work. She realised, whenever she felt pain because of her colleague's unreasonable expectations, that what she should do was to pray for her colleague. She could not change him but she refused to be upset by his ways.

As a junior staff, she became known for her unusual quietness and calm, just doing her work so efficiently, whether anyone was watching or not. She would never give in to the difficult co-worker's unreasonable demands but she refused to create a scene or lose her cool. Soon the whole atmosphere in the office improved, just because of one junior employee who practised boundaries at the work place. The difficult colleague also stopped being difficult as he was no longer getting any attention. Everyone started to follow Pearl's good example.

Critical Attitudes

Stress is often caused by working for or with someone who is super-critical. As with difficult colleagues, the best way to solve this problem is by limiting their powers and influence on us. Do not allow their critical attitude to destroy us emotionally. It is also unwise to argue with them. It will never work, and you will only feel controlled. The Bible warns us thus.

"Whoever corrects a mocker invites insult; whoever rebukes a wicked man incurs abuse. Do not rebuke a mocker or he will hate you; rebuke a wise man and he will love you" (Proverbs 9:7, 8).

Conflicts with Authority

Cloud and Townsend attribute some of the conflicts with authority to 'transference feelings'.[2] Transference is when you experience feelings in the present that really belong to some unfinished business in the past.

Christina just did not understand why she had endless conflicts with her supervisor. Whenever her supervisor told her that he wanted something done differently, she felt 'put down'. She would vow to herself, "He never thinks I can do anything right. I will show him."

Christina's supervisor was actually a very soft-spoken and kind man but because he was in a position of authority, she immediately thought of her father and her teachers in school who kept putting her down. They constantly nagged her about "not being able to do anything right." Her conflict with the authority figures in her life had transferred to her work situation through no fault of the supervisor. Christina sought help and soon she was able to apologise to her father and forgive her teachers for harbouring negative views about them all these years. And her relationship with her supervisor improved as well.

Expecting Too Much of Work

The corporate world nowadays works quite hard to develop a 'family' feeling at the work place. Ideally, the work place should be supportive, safe and nurturing. But the purpose of cultivating this kind of atmosphere is to support the employee in work-related ways – to help her learn, improve and get a job done.

The problem arises when someone wants the job in order to attain what her parents did not provide for her. Candy was one such employee. Her parents divorced when she was very young and she grew up not knowing anything about parental love and the love of siblings. As her company kept referring to colleagues as brothers and sisters, she thought she was finally getting what she had missed all her life. Little did she realise that the company had high expectations of all its employees. Everyone had to work very hard and no one had time to hear her sob stories or even to pass her tissue paper when she cried.

After a few months, Candy woke up to the reality that she had to look for emotional support and restoration outside her work place. She spoke to her pastor who knew her dysfunctional family only too well. Firmly but gently, he insisted that she should join a small group – an intergenerational one in which there were people her parents' age, as well as people her age and even children. Slowly but surely, she had her emotional needs met through this group as they did their best to love her with the love of Jesus. Once Candy learned to receive and give love, she performed much better at work. She realised that she was wrong to expect so much of the work place.

Taking Work-related Stress Home

The single woman should have a place that she can call 'home' which is separate from work. It may be her own house or even just a room she rents. But every day when she leaves her office to go home, she should leave her work-related stress in the office and not take it home. If she lives on her own, taking work-related stress home stops her from enjoying a change of pace and activity. If she continues to think and worry about work, and even continues to work after she goes home, it is like working overtime indefinitely. We have already discussed the dangers of working too much overtime. If the single woman shares an apartment with others and she takes work-related stress home, it is highly likely that it will adversely affect the relationships in the apartment.

Disliking Your Job

If you find yourself disliking your job, you need to search for the reason. We have demonstrated in the preceding paragraphs that we must take responsibility for our work, have clear boundaries, and not allow other people's overly critical attitudes or unrealistic expectations to affect our emotions.

A very common reason why people do not like their jobs is that they feel trapped in one way or another. Marianne lived a boundary-less life. Her father was a medical doctor who wanted his only daughter to take over his clinic. She did not know how to say "no" to her father. So she went through medical school against her own wishes. She made it through and started work at the clinic, much to her father's delight. However day by day, she was wasting away. She really disliked clinical work. Nothing could change that fact.

One day, she realised that she could not take it any longer. She would quit and go where her heart was calling her – not to sit in an air-conditioned office all day, treating coughs and colds, but to use her medical training to help the poor, the disabled and the terminally ill. She ignored her father's loud protests and headed off to work for the Red Cross. She now felt that she was actually saving lives instead of just 'monitoring truants who only wanted medical leave'. Her father, realising how the change had helped his daughter, sold the clinic and together, with Marianne's mother, also moved overseas with their daughter and became a huge support to her in her work as well.

All the problems mentioned above are solved mainly by setting up boundaries at work. For the single woman, boundaries at work are especially important or it could well become the one consuming activity that swallows up her whole life. But is it possible for a single woman to find 'her life's work' without allowing work to take over everything in her life?

FINDING YOUR LIFE'S WORK

Part of a single woman's identity is her work identity – what she does for a living. In Old Testament times, most professions were inherited or passed down from father to son or mother to daughter in a mentoring or apprenticeship relationship. Occasionally, a person's special talents in a particular area were singled out, or the call or God on the person's life was noted, and that person was singled out for a unique position. Deborah who became a judge in Israel is one such example (Judges 4:4, 5).

In New Testament times, women enjoyed much more autonomy in 'choosing' a line of work or a profession. Some examples are: Lydia, a notable businesswoman in the textile industry (Acts 16:14), Dorcas, a well-respected seamstress (Acts 9:39), and Priscilla, a tentmaker (Acts 18:2, 3).

The Biblical perspective for the single Christian woman to follow in choosing her career is that all of her life belongs to God who will guide her in everything, including her choice of a career. The Holy Spirit is to be trusted for both direction and timing.

For the single Christian woman, the idea of a 'career path' is not something that she should engineer on her own. Instead, God wants us to discover and use our gifts to His glory. As the psalmist advises, "Delight yourself in the Lord and He will give you the desires of your heart. Commit your way to the Lord; trust in Him and He will do this" (Psalm 37:4, 5). God often chooses for us a career in which our natural talents and abilities can be used and it is also He who creates opportunities for us to respond to.

In choosing our life's work, we are to be motivated by our desire to use our abilities to the fullest for the glory of God. We are not to be motivated by positions on the corporate ladder, work incentives, higher salaries, or cultural standards of prestige and status.

CONCLUSION

The single woman faces many challenges in the marketplace. In order to enjoy her relationships with her colleagues, she needs to establish clear boundaries. She must take ownership of how she feels, how she thinks and what she wants. She must assess her own abilities and gifts realistically. She must know her own limitations.

The Christian woman does not have to adopt a 'hit-or-miss' approach in seeking and developing her career. The Holy Spirit will guide her and give her the desires of her heart. But she must give God her heart and everything else will follow – job satisfaction, a good career path and good relationships at her work place. Ultimately, she is accountable to Him. As King Solomon put it in Ecclesiastes 11:9, "Follow the ways of your heart and whatever your eyes see, but know that for all these things God will bring you to judgment."

11

THREATS, TRIALS AND TEMPTATIONS

This chapter will focus primarily on the threats, trials and temptations that the single Christian woman living in today's world face. Examples will be quoted from the Bible as well as from the lives of single women in Asia.

THREATS

Healthy relationships between men and woman can turn sour and even scandalous if they are left unguarded. What are the major threats that can ruin a healthy relationship between men and women even within the seemingly safe confines of family of origin and the church family? How does the single woman protect herself against these threats?

A single Christian woman who has learnt that she can experience intimacy without sex need not feel deprived in any way. If she further considers her body to be the temple of the Holy Spirit, she would make every effort to keep the temple pure and clean. She would not indulge in idle day dreaming about the man of her dreams, and fantasise about her male colleagues and friends in a way that might arouse her desires. However, she needs to be on her guard all the time. She needs to make deliberate efforts to think about 'all that is pure, all that is holy' so that Christ can rule in her heart through faith at all times.

How the Media View Sex

The biggest threat to the biblical perspective of sex comes from the media, especially in the not so subtle ways in which values contrary to those found in the Bible are promoted.

Chastity

The media views chastity, or sexual purity, as old-fashioned and unattainable. It constantly parades the love life of celebrities, most of whom have no desire for sexual purity. If there is one message that shouts loudly at one and all, it is the not-so-subtle message that it is 'cool' to cheat on your spouse or have as many partners as you like.

This is a threat to the biblical view of chastity as a virtue to be sought after. In The Woman's Study Bible, sexual purity is well defined as "passion held by principle." Its description of chastity and sexual purity is worth quoting in full.

"The love life of a Christian is a crucial battleground. Each Christian, male or female, must consider the authority of Christ over human passions and set his or heart on purity. Chastity means abstention from sexual activity outside of marriage and is a Christian obligation. For the Christian there is one rule and one rule only: total abstention from sexual activity prior to marriage and total faithfulness within marriage" (1 Corinthians 7:1-9).

Christians are to prize the sanctity of sex. This means learning the disciplines of longing, loneliness, uncertainty, hope, trust and unconditional commitment to Christ – a commitment requiring that regardless of what passion we may feel, we must be pure."

Chastity presupposes not taking lightly any act or thought that is not appropriate to the kind of commitment you have to God. To equate any and every personal sexual desire as natural, healthy, and God-given is a powerful lie. God does not give desires that cannot be fulfilled according to His standards of holiness, wholeness and purity. Sexual purity is one of the foremost means of safeguarding a marriage from that which pollutes, corrupts, infects or destroys – physically, emotionally, or spiritually.

Purity means freedom from contamination, from anything that would spoil the taste or the pleasure, reduce the power, or in any way adulterate what a thing is meant to be. Within marriage, sexual union is natural, healthy and pleasurable not for the moment but for all life together. Sexual intimacy is natural in the sense in which the original Designer created it to be. When virginity and purity are no longer protected and prized, there is dullness, monotony and sheer boredom. By trying to grab fulfilment everywhere, you find it nowhere.

Purity before marriage consists of giving ourselves to and for each other in obedience to God. Passion must be held by principle. The principle is love – not merely erotic, sentimental or sexual feeling. There is no other way to control passion and no other route to purity and joy. If you choose to avoid the sin of sexual immorality, that is God's ideal; but if you have already given away your virginity, the message of the gospel proclaims new birth, a new beginning, and a new creation (2 Corinthians 5:17).[1]

Romance

The media exalt romance between a man and a woman, in or outside of marriage. The message that comes across is that it is 'uncool' to be faithful to one husband or one wife. It is exciting for a man or woman to be together, even if that relationship does not last very long. This is in direct contradiction of what Scripture teaches.

Most single women would probably have had some romantic attachment at some stage in their lives. It is important not to allow the memories of such romances to live on, especially if the man has since moved on and gotten married to someone else. For those who have never been involved with a man romantically, they need to guard especially against fantasising – imagining certain men in a romantic relationship with them. Even if these thoughts appear only in dreams, it is a warning sign that the single woman's heart is not at peace and could be in danger of a longing that can get out of control.

The Woman's Study Bible gives a good biblical perspective on romance, which is important for the single woman to hold in her heart at all times.

"Scripture approves of romance unreservedly. Marriages, even when arranged, were often recorded as love matches (Genesis 24:67), and Proverbs 30:19 speaks wonderingly of the mystery of romance. Three books in Scripture – Ruth, Esther and the Song of Solomon – have romance at their centre. These books are three of the five traditionally read at Jewish celebrations of the covenant between God and His people, suggesting that they have an extra dimension – they do, indeed, picture the wooing of the soul by God. Ezekiel 16:4-14 recounts God's wooing of Israel; the New Testament reveals that God's love for the church is a romance that ends in marriage (2 Corinthians 11:2; Revelation 21:2). Romance provides a balanced picture of God's calling of the soul. The beloved is not forced to respond but desires to respond willingly to the love offered.

Romance offers the lover an opportunity to focus on responsibilities rather than privileges. Rather than dwelling upon selfish needs and what others should do, the romantic lover is ever conscious of what he or she can do to show love for the other person (see Matthew 16:24-26). Everyone needs the acts of love for life and growth.

What are some basic elements of romance? Sincere admiration must be felt and shared on a regular basis (Song 1:8-10; 2:3). Differences between men and women must be acknowledged. Romance moves beyond the needs of the lover to minister to the beloved."[2]

Single Women and Married Men

At forty, Josephine looked more youthful than her age. She was not particularly attractive but was an excellent communicator and related very well to men in general. Her male colleagues at work liked her very much. She came from a male-dominated family and was quite used to serving the men in her family. She was single and had come to terms with her singleness. As a Christian, she had slowly but surely released her desire for marriage to her God. "It's OK if I never get married, Lord. I know you love me so much and that's all I ever need."

Surely such deliberate and repeated surrenders on her part were enough to keep her 'safe' from threats, especially at her work place, where she was so well respected. Perhaps what got her into trouble was that she felt so 'at home' with men. Unlike many women, she did not have to strive to prove herself. She treated her male colleagues like her brothers and assumed, rather foolishly, that they would think of her only as a sister and nothing more.

She made the further mistake in thinking that just because her colleague, Derrick, was married, that she was quite safe with him. As they worked in the same department and were on the same team, it was quite natural for them to meet up over lunch. Josephine was just too naïve to suspect that Derrick would be interested in anything from her except her creative ideas about their work. There were danger signs that Josephine just did not pick up. He often hinted about the big communication gap between him and his wife, and that he could not talk to his wife in the same intelligent way that he could with Josephine.

As Derrick continued to heap praises upon Josephine day after day, she slowly fell into his emotional clutches. As she herself was going through mid-life, her desire to be appreciated and wanted was more intense than usual for her. One thing led to another – a 'well-done' hug soon degenerated to kissing and heavy petting. Fortunately, before they went too far, Derrick was posted to another department. This gave them time to recover from their feelings for each other which were becoming quite uncontrollable. Determined not to repeat the same mistake, he apologised to his wife for cheating on her (even though she never suspected anything as Josephine was a close friend of their family). Josephine, on her part, promised her God that she would never allow herself to get into such a compromising situation ever again.

Single Women and Jealous Wives

Wives who are very insecure about their husbands' love for them – with or without good reason – often pose a threat to good, healthy relationships developing between her husband and his female colleagues. They tend to suspect that their husbands are up to no good when they are just talking to other women.

Jane, who has been serving for years in an Asian mission field, once told me that while she and her female colleagues related perfectly well to Markus, their team leader, they had a lot of problems with his wife. As Markus was the one who took care of all the finances, they needed to see him once a month to settle their accounts. Jane and her friends would always see Markus as a group and they only talked about their finances. Yet Mary, the wife, was unhappy and this soured relationships so much that Jane said to me, "We may be single but we are not desperate! It is hard to be the victim of suspicion all the time!"

I did not have the chance to hear the wife's point of view. But here are some steps that the single women took to render this perceived threat ineffective and powerless:

1. Jane and her colleagues invited Mary to be present at the monthly meeting. As a wife, she had the right to know what her husband was doing with whom, when, and why. He was a man of few words and did not see the need to tell Mary everything as he did not want to worry her unnecessarily. But Mary soon saw for herself that the meeting was quite innocent. She felt a lot more secure and began to understand her single colleagues better.
2. Jane and her single friends got to know Mary as a person in her own right, and not as an awkward extension of Markus. She was actually feeling very lonely in her marriage. Gradually and gently, they extended love and companionship to her and her children. They took turns to take care of the children so that she and her husband could spend time alone together. In due course, Mary learned to trust them and treat them as her allies instead of enemies vying for her husband's love.

Some Dos and Don'ts

God has not called us to judge other people's speech, actions and behaviour. We can try to help them see our point of view but we cannot change them. Only God can do that. We can, however, take precautions for ourselves so that in a sex-crazy world, we can still ride above the threats to sexual purity.

Here are three simple tips which are easy to follow:

1. Don't watch a sexually-explicit movie just before you go to sleep, especially if you are frustrated and tired. Instead, let sacred music flood your whole being as you slip into the night.
2. Don't read a sexually-explicit novel at night. It will play on your mind and cause you to have lustful thoughts which Jesus teaches is just as sinful as lustful acts.
3. If you catch yourself thinking of a married man in romantic terms, check yourself immediately by telling yourself – "he is not available; he is so-and-so's wife, so-and-so's father."

TRIALS

In trying to do her best to relate well to the network of relationships that God has put in her life, the single woman must expect to face certain trials. In this section, we will identify what these trials are, why they are trials, and a way out of these trials.

Many of the trials for the single woman come in the form of thoughtless comments or insensitive questions that married people ask singles. At the surface level, they seem harmless and innocent, but can trigger a whole lot of unresolved pain, anger, guilt or betrayal about being single. Married people should try to put themselves in the single's situation and not make things worse with further comments like "What is there to be so sensitive about? It's perfectly all right not to be married these days!"

Here are ten questions/remarks which pastors, counsellors and the married should never ask or say to single women in public. A brief explanation is given about why it can be a very sensitive question/remark for the single woman.

1. When are you getting married?
This can be sensitive if the single woman has a strong desire to get married but is still unattached.

2. Why are you not married?
For the single woman who is still waiting to be married, this question is just too sensitive to answer in public. If you want an honest answer, you will need to ask her in private, not in public.

3. What is a nice girl like you doing, still single?
On the surface, this question may seem harmless and even complimentary. After all, isn't it another way of saying that she is a nice girl? However, most single women will take the question to imply that nice girls get married and the not-so-nice ones don't. Otherwise, why should it be a surprise that a nice girl is still single?

4. Are you serious – you mean, you are really not married (yet)?
This remark makes the assumption that women should be married by a certain age. It can be a very uncomfortable question for the single Christian woman who is still trying to surrender her singleness to the Lord. She may have surrendered her singleness to the Lord but deep down there are still moments, especially at weddings, festivals and family occasions, when she secretly wishes that she were married. It usually gets easier to handle these moments as one gets older, but it does not always work that way for all women.

5. What happened? I thought you were such a perfect match!
It is unkind to probe unless you know the person really well and unless you have been invited to comment on the breakup. Besides, to say that "you were such a perfect match" would only be rubbing salt into the wound.

6. Do you mean you actually slept with your boyfriend?

This question is rather like Question 5. It is uncalled for, somewhat rude and of no help to the hearer. The woman who sleeps with her boyfriend, either casually, or regularly, probably has different values from yours. She would thus see this question as merely rude and interfering. She is unlikely to feel guilty as a result of your interrogation.

7. I don't know how you tolerated that husband of yours for so many years! We didn't want to tell you, but he is a real playboy, you know.

This comment is hurtful to the divorced woman. She is probably still reeling from the shock of his many extra-marital affairs. But if this comment comes from a close friend, it would hurt even more. If we knew that her husband was a real playboy, why didn't we tell her before it was too late? What kind of friend would withhold critical information like that?

8. Never mind. You are still young. God will provide another life partner for you.

To say this to a woman who has lost her husband is insensitive. Contrary to expectations, this kind of comment serves no purpose. It certainly offers no comfort. No relationship is replaceable. If the recently widowed woman has had a good relationship with her late husband, she will miss him sorely and to suggest that she would remarry is very insensitive. If, on the other hand, she has had a bad relationship with him, she would probably be feeling guilty and would not take kindly to this comment either.

9. Your standards are too high!

This comment is like a shot in the dark. It is born out of ignorance and nosiness. Of the many reasons why single women stay single, overly high standards are seldom the real reason. Women, unlike men, get less 'marriageable' as the years go by and if anything, they tend to lower their standards with the years. If they really had too high standards, they may actually be regretting it. So to rub it in is unkind and insensitive.

10. Why don't you sign up for some online dating?
This kind of question, along with similar suggestions about dating and finding a life partner, is sensitive and should not be asked. It can be frustrating for the single woman who has tried every means, including online dating, but has still not found a partner.

How to Handle These Trials

The ten questions/remarks listed above are very common questions that singles have to answer. We can teach married people to be more sensitive and not ask these questions/remarks. But it may or may not work. A better solution to these irritating questions is to teach the single woman how to handle these questions/remarks. So some suggestions are listed below.

We can put the best possible interpretation to the question. Instead of screaming inside, try to think of some reasons for their comments. They need not be perceived negatively and in certain cases, they certainly did not intend to hurt in any way.

Here are some examples of possible ways of looking at these irritating questions/remarks more positively.

If you are still feeling negative about your singleness, you may find it quite hard to be positive about these irritating remarks and questions. It takes time and effort, and a woman who is very secure in her emotional life to be able to handle these comments positively. This is where a sense of humour is a great help in diffusing otherwise tense and irritating questions and comments.

I remember that when I was an undergraduate, I met Ada Lum who was then an Inter-Varsity Fellowship (IVF) staff worker. She was single and obviously very happily single. Although at that time I never imagined that I would remain single for long, I was very impressed by how fulfilled she was as a single person. She told us what she said every time people asked her, "When are you getting married?", she would reply, "On the first." This would cause considerable excitement. "Oh, congratulations! The first of next month?" Then, with a twinkle in her eye and a chuckle that she could hardly hide, she would say, "No, no, no. On the first opportunity

I get!" I was extremely impressed because she could laugh at herself, accept the fact that she was single, and even tease her friends about it as well.

As I got older and still remained single, people often did not know whether to ask "When are you getting married" or "Why are you not married (yet)?" They usually ask the first question when they think that your chances of getting married are still very good. It is only a question of time. The second question gets asked when they think you have 'missed the boat' and wonder why. When they think that you are past the marriageable age, they stop asking all together and change their questions to "How many children do you have?" or "How many grandchildren do you have?"

Asians have a rather skilful way of asking some key questions rather indirectly. They do not ask "How old are you?" or "How old is your daughter?" Instead, they would ask, "Under which animal sign of the zodiac were you born?" or "Under which animal sign was your daughter born?" There are twelve animals in the Chinese zodiac, so it is not difficult to tell if someone is 24, 36 or 48.

When I was in my late thirties and early forties, the frequency with which I, or rather my mother, got asked this not-so-subtle question was so great that I invented a formula for my answer. It was simply to choose an animal not in the zodiac sign, like a kangaroo or squirrel, and mention that as the sign under which I was born. My mother was very amused but her friends were not. She often got complaints such as "Oh, dear, your daughter is so Westernised, she does not even know which the animals of the Chinese zodiac are."

When it seems obvious to all that the chances of a single woman getting married are very slim because of her age, some busybodies may ask one final question, the much dreaded "Why are you not married?" Very often, they proceed to answer their own question with multiple choice answers such as:

a) your standards are too high
b) you were too busy taking care of your parents
c) you are too clever for most men
d) you put career before marriage

The quickest answer that you could give would be: (e) none of the above. But this usually only arouses more curiosity and you could be plagued with even more unwanted questions. So prepare your own set of multiple choice answers to stop these questions.

TEMPTATIONS

As long as there is life, there will be temptations. No Christian, however close to God, is exempt from temptation. In fact, the closer you get to God and the more you are in line with His will for your life, the more you will be tempted.

How Jesus Overcame Temptation

Consider the example of Jesus. He had not even begun his earthly ministry when Satan tempted him (Matthew 4:1-11; Luke 4:1-13). Jesus won the victory in that series of temptations because of three reasons.

First, He knew His true identity that He was indeed the Son of God and refused Satan's wicked insinuations, "if you are the Son of God".

Second, He knew the importance of meeting our physical needs (He had fasted for forty days and was hungry) but He refused to turn stones into bread at Satan's command because He knew that God would fill the hungry with good things at the right time.

Third, He refused to let Satan distract Him from His life calling. Jesus was born to die, to go to the Cross, in order to save all of us from our sins. So He refused Satan's short cut – to jump down, unharmed, from the pinnacle of the temple. This stunt would, doubtless, draw a huge crowd, and seemingly give glory to God. But this was not God's way.

How to Overcome Sexual Temptations

The example of Jesus is an inspiration to us and an example for us to follow, especially when it comes to sexual temptations. Keep these three principles in mind when fighting temptations in the sexual realm:

1. Know your true identity. You are complete, made whole in Christ, whether you are married or single. Resolutely refuse to believe that your identity comes from being married or from having a special relationship with 'the love of your life'.
2. Know the limits of your sexuality. God has given every man and woman a sex drive. But if this drive cannot be fulfilled because we are single, then we must take care NOT to feed it with sexually-explicit movies, advertisements, fantasies and so on. Abstinence is the best way of avoiding temptation.
3. Know your destiny. Our primary goal in life is not to get married; it is to follow Jesus, whether through being single or through marriage. The final destiny for both the married and single woman is the same – to become the "bride of Christ" and to spend eternity with the heavenly bridegroom.

CONCLUSION

God has provided a rich network of relationships for the single woman to enjoy. These include men in our families, churches and place of work. We need to guard with special care our relationships with men, single and married. It is generally unwise for a single woman to spend extended time with a man without the company of a third person. Relationships, which are difficult to control, develop in such circumstances.

The single woman, like the married woman, faces threats, trials and temptations which can ruin healthy relationships. In this chapter, I have given examples of what these are and suggested ways of overcoming them so that our relationships can stay healthy and God can be glorified through the purity and chastity of the unmarried woman.

12

PREPARING FOR MARRIAGE

In many ways, the key to a happy marriage lies in relationships – between husband and wife, in-laws, parents and children. The key to a happy single life also lies in relationships – between a single woman and her family of origin, and in fact her entire network of relationships discussed in the preceding chapters.

There is no shortage of books and videos on marriage preparation. One short chapter on this topic is far from adequate. However, the focus in this book is not on how to find a life partner but on how to live life as a single to the full. So we will select only a few key themes for discussion.

DISPELLING COMMON MYTHS ABOUT MARRIAGE

In preparing for marriage, be sure that your motivation for marriage is not based on any of these marriage myths.

Marriage Provides Complete and Perpetual Happiness

While a good marriage brings much happiness, all couples experience times of distress, disappointment and conflict. If people get married looking for 'fairy tale' happiness, it is a formula for failure.

Normal People Get Married; The Supernormal or Abnormal Remain Single

Our greatest need, whether single or married, is to follow Christ faithfully. Neither marriage nor singleness is a permanent state. Singles may get married, even after many years of singleness, and married couples may be single again through divorce or death.

Marriage Cures Loneliness

Many have gotten married only to discover that there can be a loneliness in marriage. They not expected to be lonely and if their lives revolve only around their families, there is no one to help them out of their loneliness. This loneliness may actually be even worse than that experienced by the single.

Without Sex, Supplied Through Marriage, One Cannot be a Full or Complete Person

The woman who has found her true identity in Jesus Christ as her personal Lord and Saviour is already complete in Him. He provides for her everything that she needs to help her grow to become more like Him each day. It is only the sex-crazy media that deceive people into believing that sex as the ONE thing that every normal person should seek.

ADOPTING A BIBLICAL VIEW OF MARRIAGE

Marriage is a Union (Body, Soul and Spirit) between a Man and a Woman for Life

Marriage is the most intimate relationship that God has designed for a man and woman to experience together. It is not only a physical union (something that the media constantly play up) but also a union of soul and spirit.

Marriage is a Covenant Ordained by God that is Made to Last

The Bible does not view marriage as a contract made by two people who are 'in love with each other'. It is a covenant initiated by God. In Prince's words, "Essentially, a covenant expresses a relationship that God Himself sovereignly initiates out of His own choice and decision."[1] The covenant relationship established at creation for the first marriage has two dimensions – horizontal (between man and woman) and vertical (between man or woman and God). When we think of marriage as a covenant, we will think of it as a sacred, final, irrevocable commitment, the kind of commitment that makes marriages succeed.

Marriage is a Call to 'Interdependence' and not a Loss of 'Independence'

Basically, while our contemporary culture sees marriage as a loss of independence, the Bible sees it as a call to 'interdependence'. Our contemporary culture asks, "What can I get out of this marriage? What is there in it for me?" Any relationship approached with this attitude is doomed to fail. The one who approaches marriage as a covenant does not ask, "What can I get out of it?" but "What can I give?" And she goes on to answer her own question by laying down her life for her husband and then finding her new life in him.

True Submission within Marriage is a Joy and not a Question of Equality

Eve was made for the express purpose of meeting Adam's need. "It is not good for the man to be alone. I (God) will make a helper suitable for him" (Genesis 2:18). A successful marriage does not depend on equality but on love and mutual submission. When the husband and wife think and work together as if they are one person, there is much joy and the issues of equality do not even arise.

Understand Your Identity as a Wife

In Proverbs 31:10-31, Solomon describes the portrait of an excellent wife. Derek Prince points out that the beginning, the middle and the end of the picture all focus on her husband. The supreme achievement of an excellent wife is her husband. Everything else she achieves apart from that is of secondary value. She sees her success in him. She rejoices in his achievements more than in her own.[2]

Understand the Priority of Family Over Work and Other Commitments

In the biblical perspective, parents, and not the caregivers who may be grandparents, are responsible for bringing up their children in the knowledge and fear of the Lord. Far too many career-minded Christian women are simply unaware of the harmful influences that domestic helpers have on young children. In a day when 'outsourcing' what we dislike doing is so common, Christian married women often fall into the trap of 'outsourcing' their children to domestic helpers, the church and grandparents.

PREPARING OURSELVES FOR MARRIAGE

A single woman who is actively seeking a husband will usually have a ready list of the qualities she is looking for in her future soulmate. Some of these lists are unrealistic and can only rarely be found in a man who has never been married. We cannot prepare someone else (our future life partner) for marriage but we can prepare ourselves.

Build Character Under the Transforming Power of the Holy Spirit

In giving advice about how to build qualities that attract, Purnell explains why the fruit of the Holy Spirit is so important in our lives. Whether we are preparing for marriage, or for singleness, we need first to become "a woman after God's own heart" and this means allowing the fruit of the Holy Spirit to grow big in our lives – love, joy, peace, patience, kindness, goodness, faithfulness, gentleness and self-control.

Develop Hobbies

Developing hobbies, especially in our youth, prepares us to enjoy life much more, whether we get married or remain single. People who complain of boredom all the time are often the most boring people themselves because they have nothing to interest them. Developing interests is a good way to prepare for marriage. As Purnell puts it, "Even though opposites attract, the more common interests you have the broader the foundation you will have to build a relationship that will be fulfilling."[3]

Develop Commitment, Respect and Loyalty to Those in Authority Over You

The woman who has not learnt the value of commitment and loyalty when she was single will think nothing of walking out on a marriage once it turns sour or when there is some other man whom she thinks will treat her better than her own husband. As for respecting those in authority, many women who rebel against the very idea of submission cannot accept the headship of the husband in the family, a headship that is vested with authority from God, even if the husband is not worthy of respect.

Work through Differences with Others Instead of Just Choosing to Go Your Own Way

The single woman who has relationship problems with her parents, siblings, colleagues and her network of relationships can easily choose to go her own way. But growth and maturity come when we are able to accept another person who is different from us. When we work through differences, we are also preparing for marriage.

Practise Forgiveness

The Christian way of handling differences is not to walk out on the relationship but to work through differences. Practising forgiveness is never easy. But it is the only way to heal broken relationships.

Accept Yourself

Accept yourself for who you are and do not pretend to be someone else just to attract that potential husband. Far too many women regret too late that they did not dare to be themselves during the days of courtship for fear that their boyfriend might leave them if they discovered what they were really like. One woman I know actually never dared to go to sleep before her husband or get up after him as she did not want him to see her without makeup. What a tragedy! Attracting a potential husband is one thing. Being able to hold his affection is another. Pretending to be someone else cannot last forever. Some day, the truth will come out and it is better for your husband to be prepared for the truth sooner than later.

Know What Qualities You are Looking for in a Husband

Derek Prince gives a handy list of questions that a single Christian woman can ask herself about her potential partner to ensure that he is a committed Christian:

- Does he love God more than me?
- Does he love God more than himself?
- Does he witness with the assurance that he is born again of the Spirit of God?
- Does he regularly read the Bible and know what it teaches?
- Does he regularly attend a church where the Word of God is preached?
- Does he like to talk about spiritual things?
- Does he have a real desire to lead others to the Lord and see them saved?
- Has he received the baptism in the Holy Spirit?[4]

If the answer to any of these questions is "no", it is an indication that your potential partner is not a committed Christian. A single woman who is already in love with a non-believer will easily persuade herself that she will change him after they get married. This usually does not work out because disobeying God by marrying an unbeliever and then trying to persuade him to obey the same God you have disobeyed is just not very convincing. Disobedience also reaps its consequences. Although there are instances of husbands becoming Christians after they married Christian wives, the wives themselves have often backslided and given up their faith altogether. It is much easier for an unbelieving husband to pull his wife down than for a believing wife to pull her husband up.

DATING

Change in Expectations about Dating Today

Dating is no longer the innocent activity of courtship that it used to be. These days, when a boy meets a girl on a date, there are expectations of physical intimacy without any commitment to marriage. Joshua Harris in *I Kissed Dating Goodbye* points out, quite rightly, the "seven habits of highly defective dating". He highlights the negative tendencies of dating today as follows:[5]

- Dating tends to skip the friendship stage of a relationship.
- Dating often mistakes a physical relationship for love.
- Dating often isolates a couple from other vital relationships.
- Dating can distract young adults from their primary responsibility of preparing for the future.
- Dating can cause discontent with God's gift of singleness.
- Dating can create an artificial environment for evaluating another person's character.
- Dating often becomes an end in itself.

Decide Whether to Date or Not

One of the ways in which the single woman can prepare for marriage is to think through the whole issue of dating, especially of the negative tendencies, and decide for herself whether she should date or not. Dating patterns in which a man and a woman see each other alone so often, without any intentions of committing to marriage, are a potential formula for desiring greater and greater intimacy to the point where self-control becomes difficult.

Besides, when two people have time only for each other and no one else, they inadvertently cut themselves off from other relationships of friendship which are invaluable to them even after marriage. It is also a helpful preparation for marriage to see how a person behaves in the context of his own family and friends. Inevitably, dating tends to create an artificial environment. While on a date, the focus tends to be on how to be that perfect boyfriend or girlfriend so that the relationship can continue. When potential areas of conflict, like finance, freedom and in-laws, are not discussed on dates, then dating does not really prepare a person for marriage.

KEEP OURSELVES PURE

Single women often make the mistake of thinking that "it is better to have loved and lost than never to have loved at all." This pattern of thinking reflects the thinking of a world that has gone love-crazy, with love being narrowly defined as having sex. It is far from the biblical viewpoint that we are to keep ourselves pure for the life partner whom God has prepared for us. Many single women who have loved and lost find it very difficult to remain pure for the rest of their lives, especially in their thought life. Once a woman gets used to physical intimacy, she tends to desire more, and self-control becomes increasingly difficult. Many of those who have given away their virginity before marriage often regret not saving themselves for their wedding day.

LOOKING FOR CREATIVE WAYS OF FINDING A LIFE PARTNER

Parents Exchanging Details of Single Children

In different Asian countries, it is quite a common practice for parents to 'lend a hand' in helping their sons and daughters find a life partner. They may meet other concerned parents with photographs, and a list of the qualities of their children and the qualities they are looking for in a spouse for their children. Some even go through a marriage agency to register these details. There have been quite a number of marriages that took place as a result of such parental initiatives.

The advantage of this means of finding a life partner is that parents generally know their children quite well and may therefore be quite good at finding a suitable life partner for their children.

Dating Agencies

Where single women do not have the opportunity to meet many single men at their place of work, it may be a good idea to go to dating agencies for increased opportunities to meet the right man. In fact, in countries such as Singapore which has falling birth rates, there is a concerted effort by the government to 'arrange' marriages for single men and women. Many organisations have a social development unit which is a glorified name for a match making agency.

While there are some advantages of going through a dating agency, there are also dangers, pitfalls and disadvantages. The main disadvantage is that such agencies judge their success by the number of marriages resulting from their matchmaking but do not care about the successes of the marriages. In other words, once two people who are registered with the dating agency get married, the agencies are considered successful, whether the couple get divorced later or not.

Women who are close to the age of 40 or beyond would need to be more thick-skinned than younger women if they choose to use a dating agency. For one thing, men tend to marry younger women and while they themselves may already be in their forties or even older, they tend to look with suspicion at women who are older and still unmarried. This is distinctly unhelpful for the older woman as she already feels the pressure to get married as her biological clock ticks away ruthlessly year after year. She therefore needs to be doubly guarded not to rush into a marriage just because she is afraid she may be too old to have a child.

Another disadvantage of going through a marriage agency is that it may not have much patience with the woman who may need a longer time to make up her mind about marriage. Dating agencies have been known to say to women in their late thirties and forties, "Please don't register with us unless you are serious about getting married." This undoubtedly places additional pressure on the single woman. Not only is she under even greater pressure to get married, but she would also not want to lose unnecessary money paying the agency, since these 'matches' never come for free.

Church Social Networks

Some churches, especially the bigger ones, run special programmes to help single men and women meet. While the intention is good and honourable, and the church should indeed look out for singles, such programmes should be run with sensitivity for the feelings of older single women. Single men and women should first be looked upon as who they are in Christ Jesus. The church's primary responsibility towards them is to help them grow in spiritual maturity and not to find a life partner.

One clear disadvantage of grouping singles together is that they may become too self-conscious to be able to relate well to one another. Women should relate to men first as brothers and fathers and only as potential life-partners when God so directs them. A purely singles' fellowship, except perhaps for youth and younger singles, can become more of a distraction than a real blessing.

Another disadvantage of a singles group is that when couples start pairing off, those who do not manage to do so will feel the pressure to get married even more and may be tempted to compromise their standards or make the wrong choice.

Despite such disadvantages, it is still better for the church to create opportunities for the singles to meet than to leave them on their own in the marketplace. In the latter case, the chances of Christian men and women marrying non-Christian spouses are quite great, and the consequences of disobedience to God will take its toll in such marriages.

CONCLUSION

In this chapter, we have been able to touch on just a few ways in which the single woman can prepare for marriage. The choice of the issues raised in this chapter has been largely determined by the experiences shared by my friends. In that sense, the issues are real, albeit a little skewed. The Bible contains solid teaching about what marriage is about. Understanding and obeying God's design for marriage is the first step that we need to take to prepare for marriage. Such biblical teaching is well exemplified in the many excellent works on marriage preparation listed in the references at the end of this book. A more holistic view of marriage can be obtained from a careful study of these resources.

13

PREPARING TO REMAIN SINGLE

Not many single women consciously prepare to remain single. Even if their dreams about getting married do not come to pass, not many would dream about remaining single for the rest of their lives. Many are single by default. But if there is some preparation for a life of singleness, life can be much more enjoyable and focused, instead of just passing time while waiting for Mr Right to show up.

JOYS OF BEING SINGLE

One of the ways in which we can remain joyful in singleness is to remember, with gratitude to God, what we are able to do as singles which we cannot do if we were to be married. Once again, let me reiterate that I am *not* saying that the single state is preferable to the married state. It really depends on God's calling and gifting on your life.

There are joys in marriage as well but as this book is written about single women for single women, the joys of marriage fall outside the scope of the book. Let me just highlight three special joys that I have found in my long years as a single Christian woman.

First, the single woman has greater freedom than the married woman. An obvious area of freedom is financial. Whatever the single woman earns is for her to keep or to share with others. She does not need to consult her husband who may have completely different ideas about how to use her money wisely. She is free to travel. This is one important area of growth for her as well. In travelling, we are exposed to cross-cultural situations and learn to be more adaptable. The married woman who loves to travel will have to consider her family first before she makes travel plans. Otherwise, she might feel guilty about leaving her husband and children behind. The alternative is for the whole family to travel together but this incurs much greater cost which she and her husband may not be able to afford. The single woman is also free to extend hospitality if she has her own home. She has the sole use of her own home. She can allow groups to meet in her home without getting in anyone's way. She is free to cook whatever her friends like without having to cater to the preferences of the whole family. While the married woman's sphere of influence within her nuclear family goes deep, the single woman's sphere of influence in her world goes much wider. She can influence more people.

Second, the single woman enjoys greater flexibility than her married sisters. Her schedule is her own; her time is her own to manage. She does not have to free herself to be able to spend time with a husband and children. She can stay up late or sleep in as she pleases. This is not something that she can do if she has school-going children or has to prepare breakfast for the family. One of the reasons why there are so many more single women in the mission field than families may be because it is much easier for a single woman to relocate than for a family to do so. When the single woman hears God's call to leave her country and go overseas, all she needs to do is to pack her belongings and go. With a family, it is extremely unwise for a man to drag his entire family to the mission field without making sure that his wife and children are also prepared for all the rigours of living in another country.

This brings us to the last point that I wish to make about the joys of singleness. It is much easier for a single woman to be 'single-minded' for God. Of course, single women can be distracted by many things but if she chooses to be 'single-minded' for God, she only needs to seek God's help and it will be done. For the married woman, however, things are different. It was the Apostle Paul, himself a single man, who wrote these perceptive words. "...An unmarried woman or virgin is concerned about the Lord's affairs: Her aim is to be devoted to the Lord in both body and spirit. But a married woman is concerned about the affairs of this world – how she can please her husband. I am saying this for your own good, not to restrict you, but that you may live in a right way in undivided devotion to the Lord" (1 Corinthians 7:34-35).

RESHAPING AND REFINING OUR ATTITUDES TO SINGLENESS

We may not succeed in changing the attitudes of those who are happily married. They probably cannot help feeling that singles have been short-changed, in one way or another. We may not succeed in changing the anxiety of parents to see their daughters 'settled' in life. In many Asian communities, a son or daughter is 'grown up' only if he or she is married and so parents probably cannot help but worry about how their unmarried daughters will manage on their own as they get older. But we can change our own attitudes.

Enough has been said about attitudes to singles in this book. However, two things bear repetition here. First, in our journey as singles to find contentment in Christ, we need to get rid of negative attitudes – low self-image, bitterness, anger, loneliness, self-pity, anxiety, envy and emptiness. This reshaping and redefining of our attitudes cannot be achieved by us but only in the power of the Holy Spirit. It is He alone who enables us to see our true worth in His eyes and sets us free from all that holds us in slavery to our negative emotions.

Second, one is a whole number and a single woman is complete in Christ. I remember reading a book entitled *Your Half of the Apple* in my undergraduate days. It propagated the idea that we are not complete till we are married. It also gave the impression that we are only living half a life as we are entitled to only our half of the apple. I remember finding this approach distinctly unhelpful and untrue as I grew up in a Christian home and have known, for as long as I can remember, that I am complete in Christ.

LEARNING ESSENTIAL LIFE SKILLS

The woman who realises that she may be single for the rest of her life realises that she needs to learn essential life skills if there is no one to help her. Such life skills are particularly important for the single woman for two reasons.

First, she needs to learn to make decisions in a godly way without having to depend on someone else. A married woman would naturally consult her husband in making decisions for herself and their family. A single woman, if well adjusted and connected to the host of healthy relationships discussed in Chapter 7, should also not be completely alone in making decisions in a godly manner. However, unlike the married woman who has her husband with her, the single woman cannot avail herself of help and advice so easily. If she is still dependent on her parents' advice in making decisions in her life, it would be very difficult for her when her parents die. It is therefore very important for her to learn how to make decisions on her own.

Another reason why she needs to learn life skills is because in Asia, there are certain skills which are traditionally expected of men but not of women. In a marriage, it is usually the man who manages the finance, files the income tax forms, and takes care of the car and house maintenance. The single woman cannot wait indefinitely for her man to show up in her life to do these things for her. She has to learn these skills herself or at least know where to get help.

Two of the most important life skills for a single woman to learn are cooking and cleaning. The single woman who can cook and 'keep house' well is in a better position to open her home to others. If she has these skills, she can also look after herself much better in her senior years when it may no longer be healthy to eat out all the time.

LIVING LIFE TO THE FULL

The central message of this book is that the single woman can live life to the full. As Jesus himself put it, "The thief comes only to steal and kill and destroy; I have come that they may have life, and have it to the full"

(John 10:10). Let the single woman be wary of whoever tries to steal, kill or destroy her joy. Let her turn to Jesus who alone has come so that she may live life to the full.

The fullness of life intended for those who follow Christ is lived out in relationships, whether we are single or married. Another message that comes through in this book is that in order to live the full life, we need to build strong relationships (Chapters 3 to 7). We need to learn to serve the community, our church, our colleagues and our families. As the famous Prayer of St. Francis puts it so eloquently:

> Lord, make me an instrument of your peace,
> Where there is hatred, let me sow love;
> where there is injury, pardon;
> where there is doubt, faith;
> where there is despair, hope;
> where there is darkness, light;
> where there is sadness, joy;
>
> O Divine Master, grant that I may not
> so much seek to be consoled as to console;
> to be understood as to understand;
> to be loved as to love.
>
> For it is in giving that we receive;
> it is in pardoning that we are pardoned;
> and it is in dying that we are born to eternal life.

CONCLUSION

If the keynote to marriage preparation is godliness, the keynote to preparing for long-term singleness is contentment. Paul, a single missionary, wrote these moving words when he was in prison. "...I have learnt the secret of being content in any and every situation, whether well fed or hungry, whether living in plenty or in want. I can do everything through Him who gives me strength" (Philippians 4:12-13).

Contentment is indeed the secret to living a full life as a single woman. But this contentment is not easy to come by in our postmodern world. Paul reminds us that we can do everything not on our own but through Him who gives us strength. May His ways become our ways and His thoughts our thoughts.

14

PREPARING FOR THE 'ULTIMATE' WEDDING

In the last two chapters, I have dealt with how to prepare for marriage and how to prepare to remain single. But the greatest and most important preparation that we ever have to make in our life is to prepare for the climax of history. This is what is described in the Bible as the marriage supper of the Lamb. This is THE wedding that all Christians look forward to, whether they are single or married. It is THE wedding that we cannot afford to miss. I will explain why.

THE WEDDING FEAST OF CHRIST AND HIS BRIDE

The Bible teaches that the special relationship between Christ and true believers culminates in the marriage supper of Jesus and the church. Jesus is the Lamb of God who takes away the sin of the world, and the church is His bride. This anticipated union with Christ in glory is portrayed by John in Revelation 19:7-8:

> Let us rejoice and be glad
> and give Him glory!
> For the wedding of the Lamb has come,
> and His bride has made herself ready.
> Fine linen, bright and clean,
> was given her to wear.

Jesus has warned us through various parables of the importance of not refusing the invitation and the consequences of being unprepared for the coming of the Bridegroom. How then do we, His bride, make ourselves ready for that day?

PREPARING ON GOD'S TERMS, NOT OURS

In the parable of the wedding feast in Matthew 22:1-14, the main point that Jesus teaches is that "many are invited but few are chosen" (v. 14). Those who were invited but refused to come, despite reminders, would not be able to take part in the wedding feast. If we have received His invitation to welcome Him into our lives, we need to respond to the invitation. If we have been too busy to pay attention to Him and have gone about our own business, the day will come when we will no longer be able to receive His saving grace.

Another message is highlighted in the parable. The man without the proper wedding clothes is not merely thrown out of the banquet, but is bound hand and foot, and cast into darkness where there is weeping and gnashing of teeth. This is obviously the judgment scene that Jesus repeated so often with these very same words. Thus the banquet is the celebration of those who enter the kingdom, and the exclusion is the judgment of God for those who reject the invitation of grace.

Here and elsewhere Jesus uses the same idea to warn people not to refuse the invitation, and not to be found unprepared for the coming of the Bridegroom. However, we must come to God on His terms, not ours. We cannot gatecrash into the wedding with impressive gifts. We have to put on the wedding garment that He provides for us. Our righteousness and our good deeds are inappropriate and unacceptable for such a glorious wedding.

KEEPING OUR HEARTS PURE WHILE WAITING

In another parable, the parable of the Ten Virgins (Matthew 25:1-13), Jesus highlights how we should wait for the coming of the Bridegroom. Four points are noteworthy here:

1. We do not know when the Bridegroom will come, so we must always be ready for His coming. In the parable, the bridegroom was delayed in coming. Had the bridegroom not been delayed, all of the virgins would have been ready and waiting when the marriage procession arrived, and they all would have accompanied the bridegroom to the feast.
2. The wisdom of the wise virgins consisted in their understanding that the bridegroom might be delayed. Had they thought there would be no delay, it would have been completely unnecessary for them to carry extra oil.
3. The crime of the foolish virgins was not being ready to follow the bridegroom to the feast when finally he came.
4. The bridegroom's response to the crime of these foolish virgins is severe: he bars them from entering the marriage feast altogether and, more severely, he makes the astounding claim that he does not know them.

The oil represents the Holy Spirit and the parable suggests that we must always keep in step with the Spirit and be prepared to keep our lamps burning, even after extended delays in the final coming of Jesus.

LOOKING FORWARD TO OUR ETERNAL HOME

How do we look forward to our eternal home instead of being earthbound to that ultimate landed property or luxurious condominium? The best way is to focus our eyes on heaven and all that it means. The clearest description of heaven is given in Revelation 21.

Some single women do not feel motivated to set up their own home until they can share it with the one they love. The good news for Christian women who have given their hearts and their life to Jesus, the Heavenly Bridegroom, is that He has already prepared an eternal home for them.

Our eternal home is ours forever whether we are married or not. It is our dream home which we can all look forward to.

As Ann Graham Lotz[1] puts it so graphically but biblically, our eternal home is:

- A home in heaven – prepared especially for us
- The home of our dreams – the home we have always wanted
- A home that is safe – we will not experience harm and danger
- A home we can never lose – it is built to last
- A home of lasting value – a good investment
- A home that is paid for – Jesus paid off the home for us
- A home filled with family – we will live with all our brothers and sisters
- A home we are invited to claim as our own

ENJOYING PERFECT RELATIONSHIPS

All our attempts at finding intimacy on earth will finally be brought to fruition when we meet God face to face at that ultimate wedding. We will be with Jesus, our heavenly Bridegroom forever. There will be no more pain, no more tears, and no more sorrow. All our relational woes will disappear for we will all be changed. We will enjoy eternity with our Perfect Lover whom we will worship around the throne of God. We will feast to our hearts' content and delight to be with Him forever.

CONCLUSION

Preparing for our 'ultimate' wedding is simple. Everything has been prepared for us already. The heavenly Bridegroom is waiting, lovingly and longingly, for each one of us – single or married. All we have to do is to accept His invitation. We need to be ready for Him, remembering that He may be delayed in coming to claim us as His bride. While waiting, we need to keep our hearts pure for Him just as a bride waiting for her wedding day would do everything to keep herself radiant and beautiful for Him.

Our wedding gift in that ultimate wedding with God is our dream home specially designed for us by our Bridegroom. We can never afford it but it has all been paid for – by the heavenly Bridegroom, Jesus Himself.

The invitation to this ultimate wedding feast is still open, but not forever. It is open to everyone, single and married, but a response is needed. We will show you how you can respond in the conclusion of this book.

CONCLUSION

The main thesis in this book is that the quality of life for the single woman is determined by the quality of her relationships. There is her relationship with God and there is her relationship with others – her family of origin, her church family, her colleagues, and everyone else that she has to relate with in her life.

It seems appropriate, in our conclusion, to return to the foundation of all relationships – our relationship with God. In writing this book, I have been encouraged and propelled along by a deep desire for all readers, single or married, to have a new hunger for God and to draw closer to Him.

Through reading this book, you may have come to realise that you can no longer go it alone, whether you are single or married. You need God to help you repair broken relationships in your life and to build new ones based on love and forgiveness.

If you have come to a point where you long for an intimate relationship with God, I would like to help you make a sincere, wholehearted commitment of yourself to God through Jesus Christ. Here is a simple prayer to help you seal your commitment to God:

***

> Dear God,
>
> Thank you for putting a desire in my heart to know You in a real and personal way. I do not fully understand everything about You. I also do not understand all that has happened in my life, why I made a mess of my relationships. But I know You love me and so I want to trust You for the rest of my life.

I am sorry for leaving You out of my life, and especially for not consulting You about my marriage plans. I am sorry for everything in my life that causes You grief. Please forgive me.

Thank you for taking away all my sins when You died on the Cross in my place. Thank you that when you rose from the dead on the first Easter Sunday, You overcame death and sin forever. I can now live in freedom from guilt for my sins in the past. I can now live in the certain hope of an eternal future with You.

Now, dear God, I welcome You into my life as my personal Lord and Saviour. I am no longer my own but gladly belong to You.

Lord, please teach me to love You and all the people You put in my life. I thank you that You have plans for me, "plans to prosper me and not to harm me, plans to give me hope and a future."[1] Please show me these plans clearly. Whether Your plan is for me to be married, or to remain single, I accept it willingly from You for You are the One whose love for me never fails. In Jesus' name.

Amen.

***

References

Anderson, Neil T. *The Bondage Breaker.* (Singapore: Campus Crusade Asia Limited, 2005).

———.*Victory over the Darkness.* (Singapore: Campus Crusade Asia Limited, 2004).

Aune, Kristin. *Single Women: Challenge to the Church*? (Glasgow: Paternoster Press, 2002).

Ayres, Thena. 'Singleness'. In Robert Banks and R. Paul Stevens (ed.). *The Complete Book of Everyday Christianity.* (Downers Grove, Ill.: InterVarsity Press, 1997).

Backhouse, Robert. *Classic Love: Timeless Wisdom from Classic Writers.* (London: Hodder and Stoughton Limited, 1995).

Clayton, Valerie with Jerome Clayton. *Victory in Singleness.* (Chicago: Moody Publishers, 2002).

Cloud, Henry and Townsend, John. *Boundaries.* (Grand Rapids, Michigan: Zondervan, 1992).

Coleman, William L. *Questions Worth Asking Before the Ring.* (Grand Rapids, Michigan: Discovery House Publishers, 2004).

Dobson, James. *Emotions: Can You Trust Them?* (Petaling Jaya, Malaysia: PVM Harvest Resources, 1975).

Duin, Julia. *Wholly Single.* (Wheaton, Illinois: Harold Shaw Publishers, 1991).

Elliot, Elisabeth. *Passion and Purity.* (London: Hodder and Stoughton, 1984).

Franklin, Regina. *Who Calls Me Beautiful? Finding our True Image in the Mirror of God.* (Grand Rapids, Michigan: Discovery House Publishers, 2004).

Goring, Ruth. *Singleness: A Life Grounded in Love.* (Downer Grove, Illinois: InterVarsity Press, 2002).

Graham Lotz, Ann. *Heaven: My Father's House.* (W. Publishing Group, 2001).

Harris, Joshua. *Boy Meets Girl: Say Hello to Courtship*. (Singapore: Campus Crusade Asia Limited, 2008).

———.*I Kissed Dating Goodbye*. (Singapore: Campus Crusade Asia Limited, 2008).

Holdaway, David. *The Captured Heart: Guarding Your Heart in a World of Compromise*. (Tonbridge, England: Sovereign World Ltd, 2004).

Hurnard, Hannah. *Mountains of Spices*. (Illinois: Living Books, 1977).

Johansson, Nils. *Women and the Church's Ministry: An Exegetical Study of 1 Corinthians 11-14*. Translated from the Swedish by C.J. de Catanzaro.

Kane, Raymond A. and Nancy J. *From Fear to Love: Overcoming the Barriers to Healthy Relationships*. (Chicago, Illinois: Moody Press, 2002).

Lewis, C.S. *A Grief Observed*. (Faber and Faber, 1961).

McInerney, Virginia. *The Toughest Questions Singles Ask*, http://www.christianity today.com/tcw/2004/003/9.58.html.

McLeroy, Leigh. *Moments for Singles*. (Colorado Springs: NavPress, 2004).

McVeigh, Kate. *Single and Loving It! Living Life to the Fullest*. (Tulsa, Oklahoma: Harrison House, 2003).

Omartian, Stormie. *Just Enough Light for the Step I'm On: Trusting God in the Tough Times*. (Eugene, Oregon: Harvest House Publishers, 2000).

———.*Praying through the Deeper Issues of Marriage: Protecting Your Relationship So It will Last a Lifetime*. (Eugene, Oregon: Harvest House Publishers, 2007).

Piper, John. *What's the Difference? – Manhood and Womanhood Defined According to the Bible*. (Wheaton, Illinois: Crossway Books, 1990).

Prince, Derek. *God is a Matchmaker: The Divine Pathway to Marriage*. (Christchurch, New Zealand: Derek Prince Ministries, 1986).

———.*God's Remedy for Rejection*. (New Kensington, PA: Whitaker House, 1993).

———.*The Marriage Covenant: The Biblical Secret for a Love that Lasts*. (New Kensington, PA: Whitaker House, 2006).

Purnell, Dick and Kris Swiatocho. *Singles and Relationships*. (Eugene, Oregon: Harvest House Publishers, 2005).

Purnell, Dick. *Finding a Lasting Love*. (Singapore: Campus Crusade Asia Limited, 2003).

Silvoso, Ed. *Women – God's Secret Weapon*. (California: Regal Books, 2001).

Snook, Bob. *Mirrors*, http://www.fea.net/bobsnook.

Sweet, Leonard. *11 Indispensable Relationships You Can't Do Without*. (Colorado Springs: David C. Cook, 2008).

Whelchel, Mary S. *Common Mistakes Singles Make (and How to Avoid Them)*. (Grand Rapids, MI: Revell, a division of Baker Publishing Group. Spire edition, 2008).

Winner, Lauren F. *Solitary Refinement*, at http://www.christianitytoday.com/ct2001/008/1.30.

Wright, H. Norman. *"Let's Just Be Friends" – Recovering from a Broken Relationship*. (Grand Rapids, Michigan: Fleming H. Revell, 2002).

The Woman's Study Bible, New King James Version (NKJV). (USA: Thomas Nelson, 1955).

ENDNOTES

Introduction

1 Some of the best Christian websites are www.DickPurnell.com and www.TheSinglesNetwork.org.

Chapter 1 – Issues of Identity

1 Anderson, Neil T., *Victory over the Darkness* (Singapore: Campus Crusade Asia Limited, 2004), p. 38-39.

Chapter 2 – The Search for Identity

1 McInerney, Virginia, *The Toughest Questions Singles Ask*, http://www.christianity today.com/tcw/2004/003/9.58.html.

2 Ibid.

3 Snook, Bob, *Mirrors*, http://www.fea.net/bobsnook.

4 Franklin, Regina, *Who Calls Me Beautiful – Finding our True Image in the Mirror of God* (Grand Rapids, Michigan: Discovery House Publishers, 2004), p. 13.

5 Ibid, p. 33.

6 Ibid, p. 32.

7 http://theonlinecitizen.com/2009/03mm-lee-on-marriage-and-his-daughter-dr-lee-wei-ling.

8 *The Sunday Times*, April 5, 2009.

9 Kane, Raymond A. and Nancy J., *From Fear to Love: Overcoming the Barriers to Healthy Relationships* (Chicago, Illinois: Moody Press, 2002), p. 124.

Chapter 3 – Seasons of Singleness: Widowhood

1 *The Woman's Study Bible*, New King James Version (NKJV) (USA: Thomas Nelson, 1995), p. 581.

2 In Israel during the days of Ruth, the law of what was called levirate marriage or kinsman marriage was that the nearest unmarried man would take the widow for his own bride so that she might not be left destitute. Boaz became Ruth's kinsman-redeemer by marrying her and redeeming (buying over) from Naomi all the property of Ruth's deceased husband. This was done so that his name would not disappear from among his family.

3 A term used by Lauren F. Winner in an article entitled "Solitary Refinement" located at http://www.christianitytoday.com/ct2001/008/1.30.

4 Hurnard, Hannah, *Mountains of Spices* (Illinois: Living Books, 1977), p. 67.

5 These are prayers for God's deliverance in which the psalmist finds comfort in times of desperation and despair. Some examples of lament psalms are: 3-5, 7, 12, 13, 22, 25-28, 31, 35, 37-40, 42-44, 54-57, 59-61, 64, 69-71.

6 Wright, H. Norman, *Let's Just Be Friends – Recovering from a Broken Relationship* (Grand Rapids, Michigan: Fleming H. Revell, 2002), p. 85.

7 "Overcoming Grief" in http://www.christianitytoday.com/.

8 *The Woman's Study Bible*, NKJV, p. 1898.

9 Ibid, p. 605.

Chapter 4 – Seasons of Singleness: Divorce

1 *The Woman's Study Bible*, p. 318.

2 Ibid., p. 1615.

3 Wright, *Let's Just Be Friends*, p. 102.

4 Ibid, p. 100.

5 Dobson, *Emotions*, p. 88-89.

6 These points have been adapted from Dobson, *Emotions*, p. 95.

7 Clayton, Valerie with Jerome Clayton, *Victory in Singleness* (Chicago: Moody Publishers, 2002), p. 139-198.

8 Prince, Derek, *God's Remedy for Rejection* (New Kensington, PA: Whitaker House, 1993), p. 10.

9 Ibid., p. 11.

10 Ibid., p. 41.

11 Ibid., p. 43.

12 Ibid., p. 91-92.

13 Ibid., p. 92.

14 *The Woman's Study Bible*, p. 1583.

Chapter 5 – Seasons of Singleness: The Never Married

1 McLeroy, Leigh, *Moments for Singles* (Colorado Springs: NavPress, 2004).

2 Ibid., p. 20-21.

3 Ayres, Thena. 'Singleness'. In Robert Banks and R. Paul Stevens (ed.), *The Complete Book of Everyday Christianity* (Downers Grove, Ill.: InterVarsity Press, 1997) p. 900-905.

4 McLeroy, *Moments for Singleness*, p. 17.

5 Purnell, Dick, *Finding a Lasting Love* (Singapore: Campus Crusade Asia Limited, 2003), p. 237.

6 *The Woman's Study Bible*, p. 922.

7 Clayton, *Victory in Singleness*, p. 27.

8 Ibid., p.42.

9 Ibid., p. 43.

10 Ibid., p. 62.

11 McVeigh, Kate, *Single and Loving It! Living Life to the Fullest* (Tulsa, Oklahoma: Harrison House, 2003), p. 9.

Chapter 6 – Reasons for Singleness

1 Purnell, *Finding a Lasting Love*, p. 171-175.

2 Kane, Raymond A. and Nancy J., *From Fear to Love: Overcoming the Barriers to Healthy Relationships* (Chicago, Illinois: Moody Press, 2003).

3 See Prince, Derek, *God the Divine Matchmaker* for examples of such opportunities created by God.

Chapter 7 – Network of Connections

1 Chong Cheh Hoon, "Is it too late to unplug the iPod?", *Word @work*, Bible Society of Singapore Newsletter. February – April 2009.

2 Ayres, Thena, 'Singleness'. In Robert Banks and R. Paul Stevens (ed.). *The Complete Book of Everyday Christianity* (Downers Grove, Ill.: InterVarsity Press, 1997) p. 900-905.

3 See, for example, some of the works by Dr. Henry Cloud and Dr. John Townsend, *Boundaries, Boundaries Face to Face, Boundaries in Living, Boundaries in Dating, Boundaries in Marriage, Boundaries with Kids, Changes that Heal, How People Grow, Raising Great Kids*, etc.

Chapter 8 – Connection with Family of Origin

1 Cloud, Henry and Townsend, John, *Boundaries* (Grand Rapids, Michigan: Zondervan, 1992), p. 25.

2 Ibid., p. 132-136.

Chapter 9 – Connection with Church Family

1 Sweet, Leonard, *11 Indispensable Relationships You Can't Do Without* (Colorado Springs: David C. Cook, 2008).

2 This is my substitute for Sweet's rather crude term, 'butt-kicker'.

3 Aune, Kristin, *Single Women: Challenge to the Church?* (Glasgow: Paternoster Press, 2002).

Chapter 10 – Connection with Colleagues at Work

1 In Christian terminology, the Fall refers to the highly significant event described in Genesis Chapter 3 in which Adam and Eve disobeyed God by eating the forbidden fruit.

2 Cloud and Townsend, *Boundaries*, p. 202.

Chapter 11 – Threats, Trials and Temptations

1 *The Woman's Study Bible*, p. 1904.

2 *The Woman's Study Bible*, p. 1108.

Chapter 12 – Preparing for Marriage

1 Prince, Derek, *The Marriage Covenant: The Biblical Secret for a Love that Lasts* (New Kensington, PA: Whitaker House, 1993), p. 39.

2 Ibid., p. 66.

3 Purnell, *Finding a Lasting Love*, p. 95.

4 Prince, *The Marriage Covenant*, p. 97.

5 Harris, Joshua, *I Kissed Dating Goodbye* (Singapore: Campus Crusade Asia Limited, 2008), p. 35-56.

Chapter 14 – Preparing for the 'Ultimate' Wedding

1 Graham Lotz, Ann, *Heaven: My Father's House* (W Publishing Group, 2001).

Conclusion

1 Jeremiah 29:11.